T0282234

Cat Quotes & Tales

Cat Quotes & Tales

Rosie James

Michael O'Mara Books Limited

First published in Great Britain in 2024 by
Michael O'Mara Books Limited
9 Lion Yard
Tremadoc Road
London SW4 7NQ

A CIP catalogue record for this book is available from the British Library.

This product is made of material from well-managed, FSC®-certified forests and other controlled sources. The manufacturing processes conform to the environmental regulations of the country of origin.

ISBN: 978-1-78929-632-7 in hardback print format
ISBN: 978-1-78929-690-7 in ebook format

1 2 3 4 5 6 7 8 9 10

Illustrations on pages 9, 18, 20, 22, 53, 56, 61, 76, 80, 88, 102, 106, 118, 127, 129, 133, 140, 150, 159, 177, 191 © Catherine Rowe, licensed by Jehane Ltd 2024

All other illustrations from shutterstock.com

Designed and typeset by Claire Cater
Printed and bound by CPI Group (UK) Ltd, Croydon, CR0 4YY

www.mombooks.com

To my precious *trois petits chats*, thank you for all your help and inspiration. As always. I am like the cat who has the cream with you three.

Contents

Introduction

No one knows exactly when or how the cat first appeared on Earth. Most agree, however, that the cat's most ancient ancestor was almost certainly a weasel-like animal called *Miacis*, which lived between 40 and 50 million years ago.

Miacis is believed by many to be the common ancestor of all land-dwelling carnivores – so dogs as well as cats. But evidence suggests that the first cat appeared millions of years before the first dog.

Perhaps the best known of the prehistoric cats is *Smilodon*, the sabre-toothed cat sometimes called a sabre-toothed tiger. This formidable animal hunted throughout much of the world but became extinct long ago.

So, how did ancestors of our precious furball make the transition from tiger to ruler of our homes and hearts? Research into the genetic composition of house cats and their ancestors concluded that all domestic moggies have a common ancestor, the African wildcat called *Felis silvestris lybica*, or 'cat of the woods'.

Fossil records from early human settlements show the coexistence of these wildcats and humans, but recent evidence suggests that it wasn't until around 10,000 years ago that the way we viewed cats began to change, with the finding of a cat in Cyprus who had been buried with its owner.

Definitions of a cat

[kæt] *noun*

1. The furry little sociopath who rules the world.
2. A purring bundle of joy capable of inflicting blood wounds with play.
3. A best friend that loves you but won't admit it.
4. A ninja in a fur bodysuit with knives concealed in the paws.

See also: catnipulation (*noun*) – the technique used by cats to get whatever they want.

'Caturday, my favourite day of the week.'

Lily Rose

The two main theories surrounding the domestication of cats are that either the original *Felis sylvestris lybica* was deliberately tamed and selected for friendliness; or the period's many farming communities (with their abundance of mice and rodents attacking the grain supplies) appealed to the wildcats. Gradually, through mutual consent, cats became 'tolerated' by humans and gradually diverged from their 'wild' relatives through natural selection and adaptation to hunting the vermin found around human settlements.

'It doesn't matter whether a cat is black or white, as long as it catches mice.'

Deng Xiaoping

Slowly, over time, certain cats would have become used to humans too, learning that by being closer to people they would get easy access to prey.

Domestication of the cat

Felis catus are small, carnivorous members of the family Felidae and the only member of that family that join humans in domesticated bliss. However, it's widely thought that as a species they shouldn't be considered 'domestic' because their behaviour and form is still so like that of their wildcat ancestors. They are still perfectly capable of surviving in the wild and some cat behaviour and traits, including their love of warmth and of sunning themselves, stem from when their wildcat ancestors lived in desert climates.

It would be more accurate to say that cats are 'tame', because they have kept their wild instincts, they can still survive without us and are naturally solitary animals. But they can show affection towards us and actively choose to come back for lap cuddles and chin strokes. That's quite a compliment.

Definitions of a cat owner

[kæt ˈəʊne(r)] *noun*

1. A person who has accepted a lifelong commitment to being at the beck and call of a furry overlord.
2. A passionate collector of cat toys and trinkets.
3. Someone fluent in the language of purr and meow.
4. A person who doesn't actually *own* a cat.
5. A member of staff.
6. A professional warm-lap provider.

The cat who's got the cream . . .

What is it about these unreasonable, sulky, stubborn, gloriously sassy wild creatures that we love? According to some psychologists, the answer is simple: they can live in the moment, a feat that is so hard for us humans to do. When they allow us to stroke them, they register our tactile presence in a deeply felt way: then they start to purr. They may roll onto their backs and expose their vulnerability. They might lean in and seek out our hand for continuous touch. But they are saying: 'I am focused on receiving this attention and nothing else.'

'We're all mad here. I'm mad. You're mad,'
said the Cat.

'How do you know I'm mad?' said Alice.

'You must be,' said the Cat,
'or you wouldn't have come here.'

Lewis Carroll, *Alice in Wonderland*

In that delightful moment when our fingers are rhythmically caressing their velvet fur, they aren't remembering when we went on holiday and left them with a stranger or when we forgot to feed them or clean out their litter tray (insert your own unsavoury moment here); they have let go of all that. They're just accepting the love, being with us, right here, right now. Purrr-fect.

Cat Legends

'In ancient times, cats were worshipped as gods; they have not forgotten this.'

Terry Pratchett

The shared history of cats and humans dates back millions of years: whether spiritual or practical, it seems there is an opinion of our feline friends in every culture. As we will see in Chapter 2: The Magical Meow, they take the starring role in many superstitions, but let's focus first on their role in legends from yesteryears . . .

The Norse goddess Freyja, deity of love, fertility, war, wealth, divination and magic, rode in a chariot pulled by two giant grey cats given to her by the god Thor. So commanding was the queen bee of the gods' presence as she rode into Valhalla with her two fur babies, farmers would leave out offerings for all the local kitties (referred to as 'fairy cats') in the hope that this would bring a successful harvest.

According to Viking legends, some moggies might have sailed about the Viking ships as well, helping to protect the food supply from disease-bearing vermin.

During Viking wedding ceremonies, it was a common practice to gift the bride a kitten to bring her new family good blessings with the gods and good luck with their harvest too. Hands up for bringing that tradition back!

Greek mythology tells of how the goddess Hecate assumed the form of a cat to escape the monster Typhon. Afterwards, she extended special treatment to all cats.

A cat god called Li Shou appears in the Chinese *Book of Rites* and was worshipped by farmers because she protected the crops from being eaten by rodents; she is associated with protection, fertility and abundant crops.

Apart from being a fertility goddess, Li Shou is also part of a creation tale in ancient Chinese mythology. It is believed that Li Shou was chosen as the creature given the almighty task of running the world. But cats had no interest in such a responsibility and Li Shou wanted to lounge in the sun and chase butterflies (we hear you). She told the gods that she was not interested in such a chore and nominated humans instead.

Ai Apaec (not to be confused with the villain in the Marvel Universe), was a god of the pre-Inca civilization known as the Mochica. He was often depicted as an old man with a wrinkled face, long fangs and cat-like whiskers and was said to have evolved from one of the ancient cat gods.

In ancient Poland, the Ovinnik appeared in the form of a black cat and was worshipped by many farming families because he watched over domestic animals and chased away evil-natured ghosts and mischievous fairies. (Like most creatures of Slavonic mythology, the Ovinnik was great until you didn't appreciate him or give him what he needed – he'd then do things like make mischief that could have tragic results.)

Ceridwen, the beautiful Welsh goddess of wisdom and mother of the famous bard Taliesin, was attended by white cats who carried out her orders on Earth.

M marks the spot

In another legend, Muhammad rested his hand lightly on the brow of his favourite breed of cat, a tabby. As a result, so the legend runs, tabbies have borne an 'M' mark on their foreheads ever since.

A Christian legend, however, suggests that it was the Virgin Mary who, as a reward to the cat that purred the infant Jesus to sleep, ordained that all tabbies should henceforth wear a letter 'M' on their foreheads.

The cat is the fourth animal symbol in the twelve-year cycle of animals that makes up the Vietnamese zodiac. The most recent Year of the Cat began on 22 January 2023 and concluded on 9 February 2024. Those born under the sign are said to be blessed with intelligence, patience and a quick and flexible mind.

10 reasons why you have to own a cat

1. Cats are always interested in whatever you are interested in.
2. Cats don't care if you don't feel like going out.
3. Cats never criticize.
4. Cats don't mind what you watch on TV.
5. Cats won't judge your drunk texts.
6. Cats don't talk back.
7. It's easy to make dinner for a cat.
8. Cats don't need to be walked.
9. Cats don't run up huge telephone bills.
10. Cats don't mind if you call them silly names.

Kitsch cat

The kitsch Japanese figurine of the cat that looks like it's waving to you is called Maneki Neko, or 'the beckoning cat': the goddess of good luck and prosperity. Japanese people believe that cats bring good luck to their owners and that the sound of their bells attracts good fortune.

Now you can get the Maneki Neko in a rainbow of

colours for different types of luck. The famous golden cat for prosperity is still the most popular but there is also a pink one for those hoping for more luck in their love lives and a blue one if you are worried about traffic safety.

A Japanese proverb, '*Neko wo koroseba nanadai tataru*' ('If you kill a cat, it will haunt your family for seven generations') is based on the belief that cats have a longevity beyond human lives – oh, and that if you look after them, they will look after you!

Other cats in mythology

Not all cats in Japanese mythology were seen as gentle, flourishing creatures, however. Bakeneko is considered a demon cat and behind his appearance as a big-tailed tomcat he is a fearsome monster capable of flying, mutating, throwing fireballs and walking on two legs like a human. As you do.

In Hindu mythology, the goddess Shasti rides a cat. They also believe that the way cats carry their kittens from one home to the next is like a soul's journey of reincarnation.

'When Rome burned, the emperor's cats still expected to be fed on time.'

Seanan McGuire

Cats in ancient Egypt

About 5,000 years ago, cats were accepted members of the households of Egypt; indeed, the Egyptians were the first civilization to tame the cat. Many of the breeds we know today have evolved from these ancient cats. For the Egyptians, however, the cat was more than just a pet; they were used to hunt fish and birds, and to keep down the rat and mice populations that infested the grain stocks along the Nile.

Egyptians considered the cat so valuable that laws were created to protect it, and this reverence of the feline developed into a cult of cat worship that would last for more than two 2,000. To kill a cat was a crime punishable by death.

The Egyptians also had strict laws prohibiting the export of their cats, but their value as rat-catchers meant that cats were taken by the Greeks and Romans to most parts of Europe. Domestic cats could also be found in

India, China and Japan, where they were prized as pets as well as rodent-catchers.

Sacred cats were kept in sanctuaries in ancient Egypt, and carefully tended to by priests who watched them day and night. The priests made their famous predictions by interpreting even the smallest movement of the cats; a purr or even a twitch of a whisker may have been observed and noted. The temple cats wore heavily jewelled collars and were treated like royalty.

The cat goddess Bastet became one of the most sacred figures of worship. She was represented as having the head of a cat.

'The ancient Egyptian word for cat was *mau*, which means "to see".'

Unknown

Cats were said to be able to control the moon's movement and to protect the dead, and were given total authority over the royal houses at night because of their ability to see in the dark.

When a cat belonging to an ancient Egyptian family

died, the entire household would embark on an extreme beauty regime by removing their eyebrows as a sign of mourning. Once regrowth began, the period of sorrow would be over.

'There's a reason cats were near deity in ancient Egypt. Dogs may be loyal, but cats are smart. You can take the cat out of Egypt, but you can't take Egypt out of the cat.'

Kirsten White

Ra, both the supreme deity and the sun god of the ancient Egyptians, was believed to battle each night with the Serpent of Darkness, for which he would adopt the form of a tomcat.

After a cat's death, its body was mummified and buried in a special cemetery alongside embalmed mice, which the cat could eat in the afterlife. In the excavated remains of one temple, uncovered in the nineteenth century, the preserved bodies of more than 300,000 cats were discovered.

The ancient Egyptians were so protective of their

sacred cats that they would send soldiers to recover those that had been snatched by the traders. Consequently, the Phoenicians needed to set up breeding catteries far from Egypt's sphere of influence. The most likely place for these would have been around the North Atlantic coast of Brittany.

Phoenician traders first acquired cats during a revolt in 1100 BC, which resulted in Phoenician independence from Egypt. Smuggling abroad the cats they had seized must have been dangerous, because the Egyptian penalty for exporting cats was death.

Cats in history

Phoenician cargo ships are thought to have brought the first domesticated cats to Europe around 900 BC, when their coastal trade routes included Gaul (France), and Kernow (Cornwall, England), from where the traders acquired tin for the manufacture of weaponry. While they were items of trade, the cats also suppressed pest numbers on board ships. So began the migration of these tenacious animals around the world, and their evolution into thirty-seven different species within the Felidae family.

The fate of the cat in Europe changed radically during the Middle Ages, when it became an object of superstition. Cats were associated with the feminine; and, during a time when everyone was dying and no one was happy, women were pinned as the scapegoats for everything – being burned at the stake for 'witchcraft'. Hence the correspondence between witches and cat ownership. Oh, you caught the Black Death? Probably because you have a cat.

Essentially, it was thought that cats were the spawn of the devil. And not just in a 'please stop sitting on my head'-type way – more like, 'I suddenly believe in a crazy and unjustified theory that cats have been sent to Earth to spread evil by witches and the devil.' Cat ownership often served as proof when people were suspected of practising witchcraft, and both cat and woman would be put to death. Rude.

With the cat population dwindling, the numbers of disease-carrying rats increased – a factor that contributed greatly to the spread of plagues and other epidemics throughout Europe. But, you know, people still blamed the cats . . .

By the seventeenth century, the cat had begun to regain its former place as a companion to people and a pest controller. Many writers, particularly in France and England, began to keep cats as pets and write about their good qualities. It became fashionable to own and breed cats, especially the long-haired varieties. By the late 1800s, cat exhibitions were being held in Britain and the United States, and cat fanciers' organizations were established.

It is not clear when cats were first introduced to America. Anecdotal evidence suggests that cats were brought over by the pilgrims on the *Mayflower*. In 1868, the 'Cat System' was introduced in London, whereby three cats were employed as mousers in public buildings at a salary of two shillings (10 pence/12 cents) per week. The first breeding pair of Siamese cats arrived in England in 1884. In England, the first formal cat show was held in 1871; in America, in 1895.

In ancient times, a criminal's punishment sometimes included having his tongue cut out; the tongue was often fed to the sovereign's pets. This is perhaps the origin of the question, 'Cat got your tongue?'

The Norwegian Forest Cat (NFC) is one of the most famous 'magical' cat breeds born from the legend of long-haired fairy cats who lived in the mountains. Old Norse mythology describes these cats as being so big and so heavy that not even the gods were able to lift them and a particular popular story sees Thor, the strongest of all the gods, losing in a show of strength to sea serpent Jormungandr. But only because Jor was disguised as a Norwegian Forest cat.

People from certain cultures believed that these cats, also called *skogkatt* (literally translates to 'forest cat') were actually goblins or fairies in disguise because of their large and mystical appearance.

In the 1950s King Olaf V of Norway declared the Norwegian Forest cat the country's national cat and they have been popular pets ever since. Maine Coons are descendants of the Forest cats and while NFC's love people and do make good pets, they also demand a lot of attention. Just to warn you.

But on the plus side, if you did have an NFC as a pet and find yourself snuggled on the sofa with them, why not try seeing if you can be transported to another world by looking into their eyes? According to some legends, if you stare long enough into the eyes of the Norwegian Forest cat, you can actually see into a magical world full of fairies, goblins, and other magical creatures.

Heard the one about the sea witch? Some superstitious sailors believe that cats can cause storms at sea, from the legend of a woman who went on a sailing trip with her beloved. The fisherman and his fiancé, who was also a witch, were having a merry time until the rest of the crew decided that having a woman on board was bad luck.

While they were sailing, the crew became more and more agitated by her and wanted her thrown overboard (a bit harsh) and so she ended up cursing them and causing a huge storm to wreck the ship.

Legend tells that she now haunts the seas as a cat with four eyes. Years after her demise, her fisherman lover continued to throw her morsels of food to calm her and satisfy her so that she would never do the same thing again, and some sailors still throw fish overboard as an offering to her before they set sail.

'In nine lifetimes, you'll never know as much about your cat as your cat knows about you.'

Michel de Montaigne

In ancient Scottish and Irish folklore, it was believed that a huge black cat with a white mark on its chest wandered the countryside at night looking for souls to steal.

This cat was called the *cat-sìth* and in order to distract the cat at funerals, people would use catnip or loud music to protect the dead man's soul. They wouldn't light a fire in the dead person's room either for fear of attracting the *cat-sìth* who liked warmth and shelter and would be attracted by the fire.

According to legend, the *cat-sìth* was a witch in disguise who could turn into a cat but on the ninth time of doing so, became a cat forever.

Every year on the Gaelic festival of Samhain, some farmers would leave out saucers of milk and they would be blessed by the *cat-sìth*. But those that didn't would be cursed and see their cow's milk dry up.

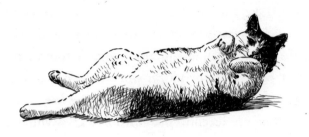

The Magical Meow

'I believe cats to be spirits come to
earth. A cat, I am sure, could walk on
a cloud without coming through.'

Jules Verne

The spiritual meaning of cat encounters

Cats have long been regarded as energetically and
spiritually enlightened animals, respected for their
independence and intuition. They can keep our homes

clear of negative energies if we respect the energetic link that connects us to all creatures. In the same way, our ancestors acquired vast knowledge from animals, who had much to teach us about survival and sustenance of the land. But what, specifically, are the implications of finding yourself in the presence of a cat?

The key to unravelling the spiritual meaning of a cat encounter is to listen to your own inner wisdom.

A cat walking towards you. A cat walking directly towards you, rather than simply crossing your path, is generally thought to be bringing you luck. And good luck at that! (Note to self: if this happens, buy a lottery ticket.)

A cat walking away from you. A cat walking from behind and away from you is believed to be taking your good fortune away with it. But don't despair: another theory is that the mystic mog is leading or guiding you towards something bigger and better around the corner!

A cat washing its face. One folklore interpretation suggests that when a cat washes its face within view of a group of young girls, the first of them to spot it is expected to be the first to wed. So, if you're looking for love, start looking for cleaning cats.

A cat crossing your path. This can be seen as a metaphor for the future, with the road symbolizing days, weeks, months or even years ahead. A cat that positions itself on your path may be symbolically placing itself on your timeline, which can be helpful when interpreting the message – does it relate to something you have been trying to avoid that you need to think about right now?

'When a black cat crosses your path, follow it. Understand the knowable unknown.'

Lionel Suggs

A black cat crossing your path. This relates to luck and forms the basis of a long list of superstitions that vary depending on where you live in the world and what direction the cat is moving. Ready? Here is the list:

- In most parts of Western Europe, a black cat crossing your path is considered bad luck.

- In Germany, Ireland and the United Kingdom, it depends on the direction that the moggie moves – from left to right, it's considered to be a sign of good luck but if it's travelling from right to left it's bad luck. So pay attention!

- If a black cat crosses your path, quickly look up to the sky and before you return home from your journey you may find some money.

- If a black cat visits your house, then good fortune will visit you – the blacker the luckier.

- If you meet a black cat while travelling along the street, you should return home and begin your journey again – otherwise you will find bad luck.

- If a black cat starts to cross your path but turns back halfway, you will have bad luck. However, the cat that continues across your path will bring you good luck. Keeping up at the back?

Colourful-coated cats

Cats are one of the few animals whose symbolism is linked closely to our emotions by the colour of their coat. So, what do the different colours mean?

'The purity of a person's heart can be
quickly measured by how they regard cats.'

Anonymous

Black cats. Black cats have been associated with evil
since pre-Christian times. Hebrew and Babylonian
folklore, for example, compared the cat to a coiled
serpent – the association is perhaps unlikely until one
considers a cat's favourite position, curled up by a
hearth or fire. However, it was in Europe during the
Middle Ages that these cats became synonymous with
witches, witchcraft, black magic and bad luck. More
recently, the black cat has been a symbol of both the
Wicca religion and some anarchist political parties.

In certain countries, black cats are considered lucky
and white cats are the harbingers of bad luck. The
persecution of witches in seventeenth-century France
brought in its wake the persecution of their supposed
'familiars': cats, especially black ones. Although
Cardinal Richelieu (1585–1642), Minister of State to
Louis XIII, was one of the most powerful men in the
country, he harboured a great fondness for cats. It is

this, perhaps, that led to the legend that the cardinal's black cat, Lucifer, used to smuggle cats on to ships bound for North America. If a black cat keeps turning up at your house, it's generally considered to be a positive omen. If you have a beautiful black cat as a pet, of course, you're already very lucky.

There is some truth in every superstition, including those concerning cats. In the seventeenth century, King Charles I of England was known to love his black cat very much and even had his royal guards ensure that his cat remained safe. The day after his cat died, the king was arrested during the English Civil War. The king's supporters claimed that his cat was the source of this misfortune and rumours became widespread. It did not help the black cat's cause when one was seen crossing the path of a crew of British sailors who would eventually be lost at sea in the late-eighteenth century.

Ginger cats. Gingers are always male, so seeing a ginger cat could be a message around masculine energy or traditionally masculine character traits. Ginger cats are also seen as bringing good news in relation to business or financial matters. If you've been waiting for news about a job interview or pay rise, seeing a ginger ninja spring into your life could be a good sign!

Grey cats. Grey/silver/blue and lilac are colours often associated with the psychic realm; so if you've recently seen a grey cat, you might be receiving a message in a dream soon. It might also mean that the dream could be bringing you valuable insights into your life, so you might want to keep a notebook close by to record details as soon as you wake up.

Grey cats can also be linked to uncertainty or ambiguity (like the situation of having a 'grey area'), so you might see one when you are unsure about something in your life. Seeing a cat with grey fur can act as a reminder that you need to follow your intuition.

Because silver is a valuable metal (silver has a cosmic value too), in some cultures a silver/grey cat is given to newlyweds to bring them good fortune and a long life together.

Grey cats are sometimes considered a symbol of an 'old soul'. Some believe that the grey cat is a reincarnation of some of the oldest souls in the universe.

Most popular cat names according to colour

Black: Raven, Sooty, Ebony,
Wednesday and Cinder

White: Snowy, Frost, Vanilla,
Snowflake, Pearl, Luna

Black and white (tuxedo): Felix,
Bond, Sylvester, Oreo, Zorro

Ginger: Phoenix, Sunspot, Mars,
Blaze, Firefly, Butterscotch

Grey: Cinders, Gandalf, Misty, Opal, Ash, Smokey

Tabby: Marbles, Tigger, Tabitha,
Cheetah, Harlequin

Tortoiseshell: Pebbles, Autumn,
Patches, Java, Phoenix

Tabby/brown cats. Brown is often connected to domestic life, earthiness, being grounded and feminine energy. A tabby cat is usually a symbol of purity and loyalty; and seeing a brown or tabby cat is usually believed to be a sign that good news is on the way – most likely relating to your home life.

Brown cats are linked to natural, wholesome and authentic qualities while also embodying stability and protection.

White cats. White as a colour is often associated with innocence and purity, which links to white cats being acknowledged as representing peace, healing and clarity. White cats are a symbol of healing, too, with the white colour reflecting the white light of spiritual energy.

Many people also believe in the superstitious connection between white cats and the full moon, which is seen to bring positive energy, happiness and good health to the home.

There are also some kooky white-cat superstitions that vary across the world. Some of our favourites include:

- In the UK, some people believe that white cats hold a grudge for years and it's considered extremely unwise to offend or annoy a white kitty. Offering kindness to a white cat by giving them treats when you see them will bring you good luck for the rest of the day.

- In North America, superstitious mothers won't leave their newborns with a white cat as they believe the cat would feel threatened by the purity and innocence of the child and place a curse on the baby.

Conversely, in some Mediterranean countries, if a white cat takes a liking to your child, it's thought that they will grow up to be a good and great achiever.

Psychic cats

Cats have occasionally been observed becoming unusually agitated in the hours before an earthquake, scratching at doors or hurrying outside. The ancient Chinese used to rely on cats to predict natural disasters. It is not known exactly where these powers of prediction come from, but it is thought that cats may have a sensitivity to static electricity, magnetic fields or faint tremors that humans do not – and that it is this sensitivity that prompts their unusual behaviour.

Curious cats

Does curiosity kill the cat? Well, one would hope not, but cats' natural curiosity can certainly get them into a lot of trouble. Whether being locked into suitcases and travelling on planes or climbing on to precarious shelves and knocking over ornaments, cats certainly know how to get up to mischief. Then there is their fascination with moving objects – unguarded fans and cats are a definite no-no.

'Curiosity killed the cat, but satisfaction brought it back.'

Ancient proverb

However, according to tests performed by US veterinarian Donald Adams, cats possess a high level of intelligence and can remember problem-solving strategies to think their way around situations.

Cats have excellent memories, and this particularly applies to inherited knowledge or things learned long ago but no longer used, such as how to hunt or defend themselves.

The power of the purr

The purr of a cat creates vibrations within a low-range frequency of 20–140Hz that provides therapeutic healing powers relating to many aspects of health:

Stress relief. Stroking a purring cat can be calming, with the movement and sound perfectly synchronized for the release of endorphins.

Healthy heart. People who own cats are at significantly lower risk (in some research, up to 40 per cent lower) of having a heart attack.

Muscle miracles. The vibrations of a purr are reportedly linked to healing muscle, ligament or tendon injuries.

Blood pressure. Cat owners who regularly stroke and hear their cat purr have lower blood pressure.

Bone strength. A purr with a frequency between 25 and 50Hz is best for promoting bone strength.

Nine lives

The origin of the belief that a cat has nine lives is unknown. One possibility is that the number nine is the 'trinity of trinities' and therefore considered lucky.

'Good king of cats, nothing but
one your nine lives.'

William Shakespeare, *Romeo and Juliet*

Their extreme physical flexibility and suppleness have meant that cats are often able to survive high falls, which may have contributed to the belief that they frequently appear to cheat death and thus have more than one life.

Witches were sometimes said to have the ability to shapeshift into a cat a total of nine times, which may account for their familiars being said to have nine lives.

Cats and the weather

It has been said that cats can forecast the weather: expect high winds when a cat claws at the carpet or at curtains, and rain when a cat washes its ears.

A particularly abundant source of such lore comes from the maritime world. Historically, sailors were a generally superstitious group and their belief in cats' possession of otherworldly powers led to the idea of cats being useful barometers of the weather and oracles on the outcome of voyages.

'A cat improves the garden wall in sunshine, and the hearth in foul weather.'

Judith Merkle Riley

Cats that cried or mewed loudly would signify a difficult voyage, while a playful cat reassured sailors that the wind would blow in their favour and their journey would be swift. English sailors will still say a cat 'has a gale of wind in her tail' if it is unusually frisky.

In the Harz Mountains, in northern Germany, the stormy north-west wind is known as 'the Cat's Nose'.

In Indonesia, cats were thought to control the rain. To summon rain, water was poured on a cat. Even today, the Korat breed of cat, a native of Thailand, is sometimes ceremonially sprinkled with water to bring rain for the crops.

In the UK, a cat sleeping with all four paws tucked under its body means cold weather is approaching.

In Wales, some people believe that rain is on the way if a cat washed its ears or sneezes.

Mystical cat names

Celebrate the unique magic of your cat with some of these spiritual cat names:

Aurora: Short for the aurora borealis or more commonly known as Northern Lights, the magic of the dancing lights were, in ancient times, thought to be spirits of the dead dancing in the sky.

Celeste: From the Latin word for 'heavenly'. A pretty accurate word for spending time with your cat.

Bodhi: Sanskrit word for enlightenment and a nod to all the subtle ways your cat can teach you about life.

Alya: Means 'heaven' in Hebrew. See 'Celeste' above.

Bellatrix: Latin name for 'female warrior' and perfect to celebrate a fearless puss. Repeat the mantra, 'what would Bellatrix do' next time you have a tricky meeting at work.

Pandora: One of Saturn's moons and named after the first mortal woman in Greek mythology. This mystical name is both powerful and mysterious.

Ariel: Nothing to do with a mermaid that's little, this is a nod to the spirit in Shakespeare's play, *The Tempest*.

Sirius: A name that means 'seeker of free spirits', this would befit a cat who likes to socialize.

Skye: In relation to the sky and heaven, Skye would be perfect for a cat that knows she should be worshipped as a heavenly creature. So, most cats then.

Zephyr: The spirit of the west wind, this magical name would work if your cat is as forceful yet gentle as an energizing breeze.

'A cat has absolute emotional honesty.
Human beings, for one reason or another,
may hide their feelings. But a cat does not.'

Unknown

Witches and cats

Cats have been aligned with magic and the feminine since ancient times – they embody intuition and connect with the energy around them. They represent an unbreakable connection to our wildness, our inner magic and the wonder of the world. Many believe that the spirits of the deceased manifest themselves in the bodies of cats, where the cat serves as a conduit between the spiritual and the physical.

Based on faith and feeling, the idea is that cats choose their companions themselves rather than allow themselves to be chosen. Cats usually become witches' familiars; having taken the form of an earthly animal, they serve as a loyal guide, guardian and protector. Witches know that if we are willing to learn, we can gain vast knowledge through being attuned to our surrounding animal world.

'Witches were a bit like cats. They didn't much like one another's company, but they did like to know where all the other witches were just in case they needed them.'

Terry Pratchett, *A Hat Full of Sky*

Spiritual baptism for you cat

If you hold the belief that your cat is your guardian angel or spiritual protection and you share a magical and mystical connection that can't be explained but just felt by the both of you, why not mark the occasion with a blessing ceremony?

You can make the occasion as simple or as extravagant as you like, light some smelly candles, put on some soothing music and make sure you and your cat are calm and comfy. Say a poem, a favourite affirmation or set an intention; the point of this ceremony is to acknowledge and celebrate this powerful connection.

Pussy Proverbs From Around the World

'Happy is the home with at least one cat'
Italian proverb

This is pretty self-explanatory we think and should be thought of less as a proverb and more as a rule for life.

'The cat was created when the lion sneezed'
Arabian proverb

This stems from the belief that the first cat was created when other animals on board Noah's Ark complained

of mice. So God stepped in and caused a lion to
sneeze. Bless you!

**'The dog may be wonderful prose
but only the cat is poetry'
French proverb**

It's like saying dogs are okay but honestly, cats are the
masterpiece.

**'The cat who frightens the mice away is
as good as the cat that eats them'
German proverb**

We love the no-nonsense meaning of this – if it gets
the job done, it doesn't matter how you do it!

**'When the cat is away, the mice will play'
Belgian proverb**

For many people it means if your boss is off work, you
can have a longer lunch break.

Poems, Paws and Prose

'Books and cats are my universe. Both are infinitely fascinating and full of mystery.'

Rai Aren

Dick Whittington and his cat

Dick Whittington travels to London to seek his fortune. Hearing the streets are paved with gold, he takes only his faithful companion Tommy

– his cat. He meets many characters on the way and, after many adventures, eventually finds his true love and becomes Lord Mayor of London! Throw in a few songs, a pantomime dame and a dozen excitable 'He's behind you!' shouts and cheers and you have yourself a pantomime classic, told and performed every year across theatres in the UK.

Everyone knows the panto story of Dick Whittington and his cat (the real star of the show), but it was based on the real story of the Lord Mayor of London Richard Whittington. There is a statue in honour of Dick and his legendary cat on Highgate Hill in London, in front of The Whittington Hospital. According to the fairy-tale version of the story, it was there that Dick, who was fleeing the capital, sat down for a rest and heard the famous Bow Bells of London beckon him back to claim his fortune: 'Turn again, Whittington, thrice Mayor of London.' The stone upon which he rested is called Whittington's stone and there is a statue of his cat Tommy sat on top of it. Tommy, the real star of the tale, is always the most clapped and celebrated character during panto season.

Street cat Bob

The heartwarming tale of homeless busker James Bowen and his ginger street cat touched millions of fans around the world. Bob's story was told in James's first memoir, *A Street Cat Named Bob: And How He Saved My Life*, before being made into a film. Bob even has his own statue in London, specially commissioned after his death, which shows him in his signature scarf.

Near the statue is a memorial bench with the inscription from James about Bob, who he credits for aiding his recovery from drugs and who joined him as he busked the streets of London.

'He is my companion, my best friend, my teacher and my soulmate. And he will remain all of those things. Always.' The statue overlooks the Islington bookshop where James wrote his first book about their journey together. At its unveiling, James said: 'My hope is that when people visit Bob's statue, or as they simply pass by, that they will take a moment to remember that everyone deserves a second chance and that no one is alone.'

Cat-filled fantasies

Margaret Atwood wrote movingly about her cat who had dementia in her poem 'Ghost Cat' and has spoken often about her feline familiars and their importance in her life. Atwood grew up desperate for her own kitten and wrote poems and drew pictures of cats as a young child. Her first cat, Percolator, slept in the dolls' bed in her bedroom.

Atwood is now the owner of two cats and has frequently discussed concepts that many cat owners will relate to, including the way they like to sample the food from all the neighbours in the street – and have no shame about doing so. For example: 'Blackie was a con artist. He used to sneak over to one of the neighbours and mew piteously, pretending to be lost. They would take him in and feed him. Fluffy, meanwhile, was working the sidewalk beat, lolling around voluptuously, inviting pedestrians to rub her belly, and attracting treats. Ring of doorbell: total stranger. "Please tell Fluffy I'm so sorry I forgot her smoked salmon today, but I'll bring it tomorrow."'

In her poem 'February', however, we get to spend a day with Atwood's kitty during the bleak winter months, when the life of a cat seems to mirror the poet's gloomy, trapped mood of human survival at that time of year.

The chuckling cat

Emily Dickinson's poem 'She Sights a Bird – She Chuckles' is regularly regarded as one of the most evocative poems about a cat ever written. The American poet penned this poem during the American Civil War, between 1861 and 1865, and in it she describes the predatory stalking of a robin by a focused feline.

The cat doesn't catch the bird, no one is harmed (apart from the cat's ego, of course) and the happy ending is evident. Apparently Emily wasn't a great fan of cats; birds featured a lot more in her poems. But the way she describes the cat is delightful. Take the cat chuckling, for one thing, or the way she conjures the image of how the cat's eyes 'increase to balls' – of course, they already were balls, but if you know, you know.

In the final verse, the exaggeration highlights the little bird's flight, especially with the image of the bird revealing 'a hundred toes' and then fleeing on them. Obviously, the bird doesn't have a hundred toes, but Dickinson's ability to make us see things in a new light – even the simple art of a cat trying to catch a bird – is eccentric, unusual and thoroughly delicious.

'Books. Cats. Life is good.'

Edward Gorey

Wild cats

Rudyard Kipling's 'The Cat That Walks Alone' is part of his *Just So Stories* collection, which focuses on the taming of wild animals by humans. The story features a wild dog, a wild horse, a wild cow and a wild cat and the idea behind it is that all animals are wild until they are tamed by humans. This appears to be the case for all the animals over the course of the narrative: one by one the dog, the horse and the cow all seek out the cave where a woman and a man are living and offer their services in return for food, shelter and comfort.

The wild cat is trickier to tame because he is fiercely independent – to the point where he repeats a mantra of his own self-sufficiency at every opportunity, telling every character he is 'the Cat that walks by himself'. Because this is a repeated phrase, others use those same words to describe him; meanwhile, the cat scorns the dog, the horse and the cow for relinquishing their wildness and independence.

But the cat who walks by himself secretly wants to become as tame as the others. Later in the story, he ends up bringing comfort to the baby and becomes part of a family while still retaining an air of his wild independence. 'Then the Cat put out his paddy paw and patted the Baby on the cheek, and it cooed; and the Cat rubbed against its fat knees and tickled it under its fat chin with his tail. And the Baby laughed; and the Woman heard him and smiled.'

The cat maintains his idea of self-sufficiency and self-image and insists that he is still 'the Cat that walks by himself', but he has become essentially tame.

Being a cat

'Poem (As the cat)' by Pulitzer-Prize winner William Carlos Williams pretty much sums up the experience of all cat owners who have witnessed the delicate step of a cat manoeuvring carefully into an empty object. In this case, an empty flowerpot. We know cats are graceful and deliberate in their movements and this poem captures the choreography of a feline dancer forever getting into empty containers – whatever their shape or size or purpose. William Carlos Williams, in only a few lines, manages to convey the movement of the cat by purposefully continuing the image over each line. That is to say, in order to find out what happens, you have to keep reading to the next line, and then the next, in a free-flowing way that mirrors the cat. The poem conjures up an everyday cat scene to great effect, reminding us of the simple joys in life.

A cat's last days

'An Old Cat's Dying Soliloquy' isn't as well known as other poems about cats, but, as one literature expert explains, that makes it a 'half-hidden gem of a poem'. Written entirely from the perspective of the cat, Selima, it's a touching tale of an elderly cat who realizes she will miss her master when she has died and gone to another place.

The poet, Anna Seward, has Selima fondly revisiting all her favourite places as she looks back on her life and the pastimes of her youth, even as with 'feeble age each glazing eyeball dims'. It's touching that Seward wrote the poem not as a cat owner thinking of death but as a sweet old cat dwelling on the thought that when she crosses the rainbow bridge 'her more loved master' will not be there with her.

She wrote the poem in 1792, during a period where poems about cats rose in popularity in line with cats' changing status from working animals or pests to companions. In fact, eighteenth-century poems about cats were fashionable and well received, especially those about kittens, memorials to lost cats and black cats. A favourite part of the poem is the idea that Selima imagines a heaven where fish are easy prey and birds cannot fly away from their feline hunter. Both chucklesome and endearing.

The cat sat on the . . .

One of our favourite poems to recite, 'Cats Sit Anywhere' is a childhood favourite in playful prose that sums up the one fact we all know about the snuggle junkies that are cats. Born in London in 1881, the poem's author, Eleanor Farjeon, wrote lots of children's stories and poems that remain very popular today – and her most famous piece of prose, 'Morning Has Broken!' is a much-loved wedding hymn. Another favourite is her snappy and mischievous onomatopoeic poem 'Cat!', about a dog chasing a cat. Both of Farjeon's well-known feline writings have been made into video versions.

We defy you not to repeat the first verse of 'Cats Sleep Anywhere' next time you see your own feline enjoying its slumber in the most ridiculous of places: 'Cats sleep, anywhere, Any table, any chair . . .'

What's in a name?

'The Naming of Cats', published in 1939 by T. S. Eliot, is a poem about the different names that cats have. T. S. Eliot was a big cat fan and owned many himself – George, Pushdragon, Noilly Prat, Pettipaws, Tantomile and Wiscus were just a few of his wonderfully named menagerie. When he wrote his volume of nonsense verse *Old Possum's Book of Practical Cats*, his primary audience were his godchildren. It's unlikely he foresaw that his poems would inspire Andrew Lloyd-Webber years later to produce the musical *Cats*!

Coincidentally, Eliot was a bit of a Sherlock Holmes fan and possibly based his feline master-criminal character 'Macavity: The Mystery Cat' on Professor Moriarty, Holmes' nemesis.

'The Naming of Cats' is essentially an explanation for humans as to why cats are given three names – one familiar, one peculiar to the cat and one that remains a secret. There is some mystery about this final name, as T. S. Eliot states, in that it will never be known to us humans. It's a playful poem but the change in rhythm in the final few lines means that it finishes with a little drama. Purrfect.

Mogs and the moon

'The Cat and the Moon' by W. B. Yeats is a poem about the connection between a cat and, er – you guessed it – the moon.

The key characters in the poem are between the celestial and the terrestrial worlds, with the cat being a link between the two.

The black cat, Minnaloushe, is the colour of the new moon and has a unique and intimate connection with it, serving to remind readers that hidden inner beauty is sometimes only revealed by the illumination of true love or spiritual wisdom. It is a playful poem and Minnaloushe is depicted as a good-natured feline and an 'important and wise' cat who could theoretically teach the moon 'a new dance turn'.

The relationship with the mystical moon and the physical cat represent two opposing forces, one grounded in the physical world and the other in the spiritual realm. The cat symbolises the earthly realm, while the moon, with its ethereal glow, signifies the spiritual realm.

The final part of the poem emphasizes the importance of embracing change and letting go of the past. The cat, tired from its pursuit, falls asleep, while the moon continues to shine, which is a way of encouraging us to remember to embrace the unique nature of life and to find splendour in our everyday lives.

Getting hitched to a bird

First published in Edward Lear's 1871 collection *Nonsense Songs, Stories, Botany, and Alphabets*, 'The Owl and the Pussy-cat' remains a firm favourite with young and old all over the world and was voted Britain's favourite childhood poem of all time in 2014. In summary, this nonsensical poem is a tale of love where all rules are broken – a cat and an owl get married, a turkey presides over the wedding and the ring is a nose ring bought from a pig for a shilling. Just pure fun and silliness. Lear wrote the poem for a friend's daughter, three-year-old Janet Symonds, the daughter of another poet, John Addington Symonds.

Lear did not start his career as a poet but as a scientific illustrator, producing the most beautiful and lifelike pictures from watching live animals – unlike most scientific illustrations of that time, which were drawn from dead specimens.

'All I do is eat and sleep. Eat and sleep, eat and sleep. There must be more to a cat's life than that. But I hope not.'

Garfield

Literary names for your mog

Need ideas to name your cat and want some highbrow literary inspiration? Look no further, friends . . .

Cheshire: As in the Cheshire Cat from *Alice's Adventures in Wonderland* by Lewis Carroll. Apart from the fact that this cat would sometimes disappear, leaving just a weird, overexaggerated grin in its place, the Cheshire Cat was pretty cool. He was kind and friendly to Alice and exhibited all the other personality traits you want in a cat – sometimes a bit kooky, sometimes chilled, generally does what it wants.

Mog: After *Mog the Forgetful Cat* by Judith Kerr. Mog is the perfect name for a cat who is daft but ultimately loveable. And if you have a tabby that has a white bib, well, it's like it was meant to be. Mog is forgetful – she forgets she has been fed, she forgets she can't fly, she forgets she has a cat flap . . . She forgets all the usual things that are fairly important in the world of cat. But her forgetfulness makes her unforgettable.

Tabitha Twitchit: From the books of Beatrix Potter. Tabitha, Tabs, Mrs T . . . By calling your feline after this much-put-upon mother of three, you are paying homage to one of the greatest illustrators and authors of all time. Beatrix Potter is a heroine and so is Mrs Tabitha Twitchit. If your cat also has kittens, well, it was meant to be. Plus, in the Potter books, Mrs Twitchit wears fashionable clothes and is one of life's bosses. What's not to love?

Mr Mistoffelees: Star of *Old Possum's Book of Practical Cats*, by T. S. Eliot. The *Practical Cats* book is full of interesting names and characters and we nearly went with Macavity for this – 'a fiend in feline shape / A monster of depravity' – but in the end, it had to be the magical Mr Mistoffelees. You might not be a fan of the musical *Cats*, but this song will play in your head on repeat once you hear it, about the character in Eliot's book. As well as having a song named after him as part of a West End production, Mr Mistoffelees is the perfect name for your black cat who might play it cool and aloof but is deadly with dice and is a bit of card shark. Altogether now, 'Oh! / Well I never / Was there ever / A Cat so clever / As Magical Mr Mistoffelees . . .' You get the drift.

Maurice: After *The Amazing Maurice and his Educated Rodents* by Terry Pratchett. Pratchett fans will be familiar with the talking cat Maurice, who – if we didn't already give it away with the fact that he can talk – is no ordinary cat. Maurice is the perfect name for a super-intelligent cat who you know is always plotting in one quiet shape or another (although hopefully not quite as much as the cat in the book, who likes to pull off a series of cons with the help of a band of equally intelligent rats). But Maurice is kind too, and he feels guilty – so if your kitty is always doing wrong but showing some kind of remorse, Maurice could be the perfect moniker.

Crookshanks: From the Harry Potter series by J. K. Rowling. We left the grumpy Mrs Norris out of this list (see Chapter 5: Cat Tales) as our favourite feline from the wizarding world of Harry Potter is Hermione Granger's Crookshanks. Described as having a 'squashed face', Crookshanks was inspired by a cat J. K. Rowling saw when she was writing the book and who looked like he had run face first into a brick wall. So, you know, a Persian. Hermione bought Crookshanks from a shop in the magical Diagon Alley because no one else wanted him, but it turns out that he is a very intelligent cat who can detect when they are around untrustworthy folk. So, if you have a cat that is quite good at judging a wrong 'un, Crookshanks seems like the purrfect identity.

Feline love from the author world

'I wish I could write as mysterious as a cat.'

Edgar Allan Poe

'I love cats because I enjoy my home; and little by little, they become its visible soul.'

Jean Cocteau

'I would like to see anyone, prophet, king or God, convince a thousand cats to do the same thing at the same time.'

Neil Gaiman

'If cats looked like frogs we'd realize what nasty, cruel little bastards they are. Style. That's what people remember.'

Terry Pratchett

'If animals could speak, the dog would be a blundering outspoken fellow; but the cat would have the rare grace of never saying a word too much.'

Mark Twain

'One day I was counting the cats and I absent-mindedly counted myself.'

Bobbie Ann Mason

'Owners of dogs will have noticed that, if you provide them with food and water and shelter and affection, they will think you are god. Whereas owners of cats are compelled to realize that, if you provide them with food and water and shelter and affection, they draw the conclusion that they are gods.'

Christopher Hitchens

'When I am feeling low, all I have to do is watch my cats and my courage returns. I study these creatures, they are my teachers.'

Charles Bukowski

'I write so much because my cat sits on my lap. She purrs so I don't want to get up. She's so much more calming than my husband.'

Joyce Carol Oates

Cat authors

Cat name inspiration from the literary world: instead of a fictional character, how about naming your cat after a famous feline-loving scribe?

Ernest/Ernie/Hemingway
Ernest Hemingway is well known for his love of cats and so, in homage to the great writer, Ernest seems

both a serious yet potentially playful (Ernie) name for a cat. If people ask if you've named your cat after a *Sesame Street* character, you can impress them with your knowledge of Mr Hemingway, informing them that Hemster first fell in love with cats when he and his family lived at Fina Vigia, their home in Cuba.

'One cat just leads to another.'

Ernest Hemingway

When he started travelling, he was given a six-toed cat (impress people even more by throwing in the official name for this – a polydactyl cat), which he called Snowball. Snowball became his best buddy and when the family moved to Key West, Florida, Hemingway let Snowball sow his seed with all the other cats, creating a small colony of felines that lived on the estate. Apparently, there are around forty to fifty polydactyl descendants of Snowball still roaming the house. And for bonus points, polydactyl cats are sometimes called Hemingway Cats. History lesson over.

Johnson/Sammy/Samuel

Known to be a general cat lover during his life, Samuel Johnson had one favourite in particular: Hodge. We say favourite, but that's probably putting it mildly. Hodge was doted upon by the eighteenth-century writer, who would go out and buy him oysters on a regular basis and woe betide any servant who didn't like the cat. Described as 'a very fine cat indeed' by Johnson, Hodge was immortalized, complete with oysters, in a statue that sits outside Johnson's former house at 17 Gough Square in London. So, if you have a cat who likes the finest food in life, these could be very fitting names.

Dickens/Charlie/Mr D

One of the most iconic and influential writers in history, Charles Dickens sure had a soft spot for cats. Apparently, according to his daughter, when one of his felines wasn't getting enough attention because the writer was so hard at work, it would learn to extinguish the light on Dickens' desk. In 1862, one of his favourite cats, Bob, died and Dickens was so upset that he had Bob's paw stuffed and mounted on to an ivory letter opener. Er, as you do. He then had the letter opener engraved with the words: 'C. D., In memory of Bob, 1862' so he could have a constant reminder of his old pal. If you want to see the letter opener in all its glory, it's on display at the Berg Collection of English and American Literature at the New York Public Library.

Brontë/Lottie/Emily/Anne

It wasn't just a love of writing that the Brontë sisters shared; they were also all fans of their cats. Felines featured in lots of this original cat-loving literary girl gang's writing, including *Agnes Grey* and *Wuthering Heights* plus the personal diaries of Anne and Charlotte. Emily was such a vocal fan of cats that she wrote an essay in French (did we mention they were super talented?), called 'Le Chat', where she argued that cats weren't selfish and cruel, as some people thought, but were in fact more like humans than we know. And actually better than humans because they were more self-reliant. So there.

King/Mr K/Stevo

It might not be the most flattering of compliments, to name your snuggly purr machine after a man who loved to write horror stories and freak everyone out with clown characters, but Stephen King does love his cats. If you have a feline who likes a bloodbath and to bring its kill to your pillow every single day, it could perhaps be a fitting homage to name your cat after him. 'It might be that the biggest division in the world isn't men and women but folks who like cats and folks who like dogs,' said King.

Wills/Burroughs/W. B.

William S. Burroughs might be known for his drug-induced writing but if you don't hold that against him, he did love his cats. In his autobiographical novella *The Cat Inside*, we discover all the cats that he looked after throughout his life. The book concludes on a very touching homage to his last four cats: 'Only thing can resolve conflict is love, like I felt for Fletch and Ruski, Spooner, and Calico. Pure love. What I feel for my cats present and past? Love.' If you have a cat who is a bit of a creative yet loving friend, you won't go far wrong in naming it after W. B.

'My relationships with my cats have saved
me from a deadly, pervasive ignorance.'

William S. Burroughs

Chandler/Raymondo/Ray

Raymond Chandler was, of course, a hugely influential crime writer. Raymond Chandler was never far from his beloved black Persian Taki whom he called his secretary. She came into his life just as his literary career took off and was a constant presence on his desk while he was trying to write. Femme fatales and plot twists were his thing and his detective Philip Marlowe was the starring character in his works *The Big Sleep* and *The Long Goodbye*. If you have a cat that is naturally inquisitive and likes to give you knowing looks, pay homage to the crime scribe by naming them in R. C.'s honour.

Jim/James/Alf

James Alfred Wight, who is better known by his pen name, James Herriot, was a caring chap, qualified vet and bestselling author. Ticks all the boxes, if you ask us.

He wrote about his many animal exploits as a vet, but his cat books in particular were our favourites. His *Cat Stories* collection was published in 1994 and was about ten cats he encountered while working in his veterinary practice; there were also two children's books, called *Oscar: Cat-About-Town* and *Moses the Kitten*.

It wasn't until late in life that Wight became an acclaimed author. Each evening, on his return home from his veterinary practice, he would tell his wife about that day's incidents. When he told her that he would save some of them for a book, she replied: 'Who are you kidding? Vets of fifty don't write first books.'

If you have a cat that is persistent and unrelenting and loveable, Alfie might just be the name for him.

'I have felt cats rubbing their faces against mine and touching my cheek with claws carefully sheathed. These things, to me, are expressions of love.'

James Herriot

Feline Facts

'You know my philosophy when it comes to cats, babies, and apologies. You've got to let them come to you.'

Jason Sudeikis, *Ted Lasso*

A miscellany of cat wonders

The average cat has a total of twenty-four whiskers, arranged in four rows of three whiskers on either side of the face. The upper rows can move independently of the bottom rows.

Whiskers are more than twice as thick as ordinary hairs, and their roots are set three times as deep – they are closely connected to the nervous system. They are full of nerve endings that provide the cat with detailed information about air movement and pressure as well as feedback on its surroundings. Damage to a cat's whiskers may provoke discomfort, confusion or disorientation.

Further small groupings of whiskers are situated on other parts of a cat's body, including above each eye and on the backs of the front paws.

The technical word for whiskers is 'vibrissae', which suggests their sensitivity to vibrations in air currents. Whiskers are also a tool for hunting, providing cats with vital information about the shape and movement of their prey.

Food bowls that are too small to accommodate a cat's head without its whiskers touching the sides can be an irritant, as the whiskers provide distracting and unwanted sensations to the cat.

A cat's whiskers are another indicator of its mood. Whiskers pointing forward signify curiosity; when whiskers point backwards the cat may be feeling nervous or threatened.

'When I play with my cat, who knows whether she is not amusing herself with me more than I with her.'

Montaigne

The cat species can vary widely in size, but domestic cat breeds are among the smallest in the cat family. The average domestic cat measures between 20 and

25 centimetres (8 to 10 inches) tall, and from the tip of the nose to the base of the tail is approximately 51 centimetres (20 inches) long. The tail itself is usually no longer than 38 centimetres (15 inches). Males are predictably heavier than females – around 6.8 kilograms (15 pounds) compared to 4.5 kilograms (10 pounds), though this can depend on skeletal size and the amount being fed by doting owners!

A cat's brain is closer in composition to a human brain than it is to that of a dog. The region of the brain responsible for emotion is in the same place in both the human and the cat brain.

Lacking a true collarbone, a cat can squeeze its body through any space or gap into which it can fit its head. Feline whiskers act as feelers and allow the cat to judge whether they are likely to fit.

The flexibility of a cat's spine is the key to its remarkable physical versatility. The spine can be compressed to afford them comfort and sleep in snug places or elongated to enable them to leap further.

While this will come as no surprise to cat owners who have been licked by their loving pets, cats lose as much fluid during self-grooming (through saliva) as they do through urinating.

'There is something about the presence of a cat that seems to take the bite out of being alone.'

Louis J. Camuti

The tongue of a domestic cat feels not too dissimilar to sandpaper, while the tongue of a big wildcat, such as the lion or the tiger, is much rougher. This roughness serves several purposes – not only does it makes cleaning and grooming more effective, but also, in the wild, it serves as an effective tool to strip flesh from the bones of prey.

All cats – both domestic and wild – can purr. The volume of the purr can vary significantly, and can be so soft as to be inaudible to the human ear. Purring may begin as soon as a couple of days after birth. The purring sound is made by the cat vibrating its vocal cords in the voice box, but no one knows exactly how the cat uses these to produce purring, or why no other animal purrs. (Want more purr-info? Check out Chapter 2: The Magical Meow)

Quick-fire kitty facts

- A person who loves cats is called an ailurophile; cat haters are known as ailurophobes. This stems from the classical Greek word for cat, *ailouros*.

- A group of kittens is called a kindle.

- A house cat would beat superstar Olympic runner Usain Bolt in the 200-metre sprint. That's a race we'd love to see.

- When a domestic cat goes after mice, one pounce in every three results in a catch.

- A group of adult cats is called a clowder.

- Cat breeders are called catteries.

- On average, cats have 244 bones (humans have 206).

- Adult cats have thirty teeth, while kittens have twenty-six.

- A house cat is genetically 95.6 per cent tiger.

- Each cat's nose-print is unique in the same way your human fingerprint is individual.

- Around 200 feral cats prowl and hunt around the Disneyland theme park to control the rodents.

- One man made a fortune from the invention of cat litter. Edward Lowe originally designed the granulated clay to help out a neighbour who was complaining about the mess resulting from using ashes in her cat's tray. It was first manufactured in 1947. Lowe sold his business in 1990 for approximately US $200 million (£110 million).

- *Gay Purr-ee*, released in 1962, was the first full-length film to feature a cat as the star. Mewsette, the cat in question, was voiced by Judy Garland.

- Cats can drink seawater to survive (for more kitties at sea, see Chapter 5: Cat Tales from Around the World).

- The life expectancy of cats has nearly doubled since 1930 – from eight to sixteen years.

'My cats are beautifully round and fuzzy and they look like little lazy bears; they're always taking naps.'

Taylor Swift

Cat behaviours

A cat's mood can be seen in its eyes. When frightened or excited, a cat will have large, round pupils. If you're feeling brave enough to look, an angry cat will have narrow pupils.

How a kitten is treated in its early years will affect its personality and behaviour in the years to come.

It is thought that most cats bring their prey into their owners' homes to protect it from other predators, and from an instinctive urge to return it to the nest for the young.

A cat will use scent glands near its 'cheeks' to mark people as well as furniture, so make the acquaintance of a cat (and garner its approval) when entering their territory.

Cats like being stroked because it reminds them of their mother's affection. Kittens are repeatedly licked by their mother during their earliest days and the action of human stroking causes the same sensation on their fur as feline licking.

The waving tail of a cat does not signify anger, but conflict. Two warring impulses – for example, the desire to roam outside, but the preference not to get wet in the rain – will cause the cat to stand still and wave its tail.

Did you know cats can change their fur colour? Well, strictly speaking, only Siamese cats can and er, strictly speaking, only their footprints. Apparently kitten prints turn blond or brown in colour depending on their body temperature (around 36 degrees Celsius).

Isaac Newton might have calculated gravity but according to some research, he was also the brains behind the cat flap! According to research, while he was working at the University of Cambridge in England, he was fed up of being constantly interrupted by his cats scratching at the door. So he got the resident carpenter to saw holes in it.

It's said that in ancient Egyptian times, if a cat died the owner would shave their eyebrows as a sign of grief.

Studies show that cat's predominately use their left paw over their right paw. Lefties are the best. Just saying.

The technical term for a cat hairball is a 'bezoar'. That's quite a mouthful, no wonder they have to wretch them up.

To get themselves down from a tree, a cat must back themselves down. This is because every claw on a cat's paw points the same way. Or you know, wait for their owner to fetch the ladder.

'Purring would seem to be, in her case, an automatic safety valve device for dealing with happiness overflow.'

Monica Edwards

Quick-fire behaviour facts

- A cat exposing its belly is a trusting cat.

- A cat can jump five times its height.

- Cats will lick themselves after being handled to get rid of the human scent.

- Cat families usually play best in even numbers. Where possible, cats and kittens should be acquired in pairs.

- Like humans, cats can get bored – they will show their boredom through excessive licking, chewing, or biting.

- Cats will bury their faeces to cover their trail from predators.

- Cats with long, lean bodies are more likely to be outgoing and more vocal than those with a stocky build.

'All guests must be approved by the cat.'

Anonymous

Cat companions

So how do we know if a cat likes us (gulp) as their human companion? According to some cat psychologists, there is a series of behaviours you can look out for before you start to pat (stroke) yourself on the back.

They treat you like you're a cat. Which means they don't think of you as their servant. Well, not all of the time. If your cat replicates affection that they show with other cats – sleeping near them and rubbing on them –

with you, they are saying, 'Hey, you're my equal. Until dinnertime – then you belong to me.'

They follow you around the house. This is typical dog 'You are my master; don't leave me' behaviour but toddlers do it too – for them, not even the toilet is a place of sanctuary. If your puss is your shadow around the house, however: wow. You really are the cat that's got the cream.

They come and find you when you're sleeping. Or when you are having a 'Netflix and chill' moment. Cats can sometimes feel threatened by our size, which is why we often wake up to find them right next to our faces – it's an indication that they have total trust in us and apparently they find comfort in the sound of our breathing. It's not that they want to exert their dominance . . .

'My cat wakes me up at 5am every morning.
I repaid the favour at 5pm today.'

Anonymous

They blink their eyes slowly. If you want to check whether you have a content cat, watch how often they blink. According to research, a happy kitty blinks their eyes more slowly. We can mimic this by 'softening our gaze' when we look at them. No frowning, people!

They think you're their mother. Kittens make a certain kind of gesture to get their mother to release milk – a pushing in and out with their front paws. So, if your cat is doing that to you that's like them saying, 'Yo! Ma! Give me some attention over here.'

They bare their bellies. If your cat likes to truffle-shuffle and bare their belly it can be a sign that they are relaxed and in a trusting environment. It can also mean they want to play. And same goes for their tails, although an active tail can also mean they are irritated – so tread carefully.

They make the right kind of meow. The types of meow cats make are designed to pull at our heartstrings so we do what they want us to because we love them. Of course, a cat meowing constantly at the wrong pitch and not in a soothing way will get us to do whatever they want so we get a little peace and quiet. They are on to a win-win!

How to befriend a cat

Cats are masters at training us. Yup, they don't require qualifications for this; it's instinctive and therefore they graduate the moment they are born. But there are things we can learn to do if we want the feline in control to love and appreciate (we use that word loosely) us too. The number-one rule is: play hard to get.

Cats are picky companions, and it's not always easy to make friends with a cat. It must be on their terms.

Be gentle in your approach and with your touch; don't stroke them. Don't try too hard or try to pick them up. Let them make the first move. It's a good rule of thumb in life.

'Dogs like everyone.
Cats choose who to like.'

Lauren Myracle

Respecting their limits will mean your feline buddy will respect you more. Which also explains why those non-cat-lovers that exist (sadly, they do, generally using allergy as an excuse) always, *always* get the cats coming up to them and jumping all over them. They are avoiding cats like the plague, and the cats think, 'Ooh, I want to sit all over this person because they are not being pushy.'

Once you've achieved cat approval, hold your hand steady about a foot or so from the cat's face; if it pushes its cheek against your fingers, then that's the second stage completed.

Don't force the cat if it appears unsure or reluctant – remember, it all must be the cat's idea. According to research and to those who know cats, like, *at all*, cats much prefer to make the first move.

It's also important to keep your voice even and

unthreatening. If you have a deep voice, try raising the pitch a little – cats sometimes equate a low voice with the sound of their enemies. And finally, remember that cats are incredibly territorial, so don't threaten their space.

Six steps to happiness:

1. Get a cat
2. Get another cat, you will both appreciate the extra company
3. Get a third cat. In for a penny, in for a pound
4. Declare your social media status to be #catmum #catlady #slavetomycats
5. Tell your family you won't get any more cats as you aren't a #crazycatlady
6. Get another cat

Cats on the clock

How is it that our feline friends know exactly what time our alarm clock is set in the morning? And yes, they know if you are having a super lie-in today. And yes, they will be judging you.

'Garfield's Law: cats instinctively know the precise moment their owners will awaken . . . then they awaken them ten minutes sooner.'

Jim Davis

Cats are creatures of routine. This means that after sharing a home with you for even a few days, they will get to know your routine too. If you wake up at a certain time to get ready for work, your cat will figure that out. And it's the same with food. Just like we get a rumbly tummy around lunchtime, cats will judge – using internal and external clues – what time of day it is. External cues will also be 'back-chained', which means that they can chain together numerous cues to predict something is going to happen – and they can work out how long it's been since they last saw chicken in their food bowl.

'Since each of us is blessed with only one life, why not live it with a cat?'

Robert Stearns

Your cat can tell when you're waking up. Humans' sleep cycle consists of five stages, ranging from barely napping to deep sleep. Through each stage of sleep, your respiration, heartbeat and activity levels change, and you go through four or five of these cycles a night. Once you're at a light enough stage of sleep to respond to your cat's kind attentions, they'll be right in your face to help you start their day. If they start meowing before you wake up and you give them attention, be warned: they will try this trick repeatedly.

Your cat is most active when you're about to wake up. Cats are crepuscular creatures, which is a fancy way of saying that they're primarily active at dawn and dusk. Plus, their vision is best adapted for the light levels of these 'in between' times, which is why they do their hunting, playing and socializing then.

We can't imagine that many cats would fare well in an alien attack but in the film *Alien*, Jonesy, the ginger tomcat who roams the *Nostromo* spaceship in order to take care of any vermin, not only survives the first film but the sequel as well! There are all sorts of cool theories as to why Jonesy not only had such a starring survival role but also what the puss might represent . . . popular opinions include him being an on-screen representation of the director Ridley Scott (because he seems to be in every scene even when not on camera) or that he was in cahoots with and helping the Xenomorph all along and leading all the characters to their deaths.

Disney's *Oliver & Company* might feature a host of canine characters but it's Oliver, the orphaned ginger kitten, that steals the show. Loosely based on the Dickens tale, *Oliver Twist*, little kitten Oliver is found abandoned and wandering the streets of New York when he receives help from a stray dog called Dodger. And before you ask, yes the film also features characters called Fagin and Sykes.

The wonderful thing about Tiggers . . . are tiggers are wonderful things. Surely everyone knows this? A.A Milne certainly knew the loveable nature of cats and so gave her Winne the Pooh character a bouncy, excitable, a little OTT friend in the shape of a black and orange tiger. Eeyore was thrilled with this as you can imagine.

C.S. Lewis wrote seven books about the magical world of Narnia and its majestic, powerful main character, Aslan. The no-nonsense Lion first appeared in *The Lion, the Witch and the Wardrobe,* which sees the Pevensie children enter Narnia through a wardrobe. Aslan has everything you want him to have as a big cat – a mighty roar, a righteous heart and a loud purr.

Cat Tales from Around the World

'I take care of my flowers and
my cats. And that's living.'

Ursula Andress

A cat hotel

The first recorded 'cat hotel' was established in
Philadelphia, Pennsylvania, USA, and could

accommodate 100 cats in rooms that contained three storeys of shelves, each furnished with soft rugs. The lucky cats were also entitled to their own room and the attentions of a personal hairdresser, if desired. Meals – typically soup, cod, shrimps and mackerel served with milk or water – were served from plates at a dining table.

A rich, famous and fabulous feline

The late Chanel designer Karl Lagerfeld treated his adopted Birman Choupette like a pampered princess, spoiling her with private jet rides, two maids, a social-media manager and private driver. She would also get regular manicures and had her own kitty iPad. Before he died, the designer admitted that she was 'the centre of the world' for him and that her fame totally eclipsed his. 'You know, personally, I don't even think I'm that famous. Now, Choupette really is famous. She has become the most famous cat in the world.' Choupette, which means 'sweetie' in French, has been busy honouring Lagerfeld's legacy since his death, releasing her own cosmetic line and her first book, *Choupette: The Private Life of a High-Flying Fashion Cat.*

Statue campaign for Scots kitty

The residents in Edinburgh's West End are eager to erect a statue in honour of a much-loved street cat. Hugo, an Arabian Mau, was a familiar friendly face on William Street, dropping into houses for snacks, sneaking naps in beds and giving meows to all who knew him before he was hit by a car and killed.

Hugo was not only loved by the local residents, who were all too familiar with seeing him strut down the street, but also became a bit of a legend with Edinburgh's visiting tourists. At Christmastime, shop owners would offer discounts to visitors who could name the famous cat. Residents are hoping to erect a bronze statue to give Hugo permanent recognition, much like the city's legendary dog Greyfriars Bobby.

The prime minister's moggy

Larry is the brown-and-white tabby cat who lives at the residence of the British prime minister and whose job is Chief Mouser to the Cabinet Office. He is looked after by the Downing Street staff and has served during the premierships of five prime ministers. He was a former stray and was adopted from Battersea Dogs & Cats Home. He is now something of a social-media star, having acquired tens of thousands of followers with his posts – which normally feature photographs of him while visiting politicians from all over the world enter the doors of Number 10. Apparently, Larry isn't too keen on men, preferring female company, but was particularly friendly with former American president Barack Obama.

The cat from Down Under

Goldie was a kitten that was adopted by Ann Norton, who had moved from Britain to Sydney and knew that her home was incomplete without a cat. Ann soon discovered that Goldie was something of an adventurous cat and took her with her on camping holidays. 'She loved to hunt at night, although one night hurtled back into the tent at 90mph after an encounter with another animal – a kangaroo a coyote or a fox; we will never know!' Goldie moved back to England with Ann and entranced all those who met her, including the kennel girls who cared for her for six months when she was in quarantine. Goldie moved back in with Ann and her second husband and lived out her days basking on the patio in the Sussex sunshine, true to her name.

Nala the cycle cat

Thirty-year-old former rugby player Dean Nicholson set off from Scotland to cycle solo around the world, but he returned with a companion – of the four-legged kind. Having cycled through Amsterdam, Belgium, Greece, Switzerland, Italy and Croatia, it was on a remote road in the mountains between Montenegro and Bosnia that he found an abandoned and poorly tabby kitten.

With the help of local vets, Nicholson nursed her back to health and named her Nala. 'I heard a wee cat miaowing from behind me. She was chasing me up the hill so I stopped, put her in the front of my bike to take her to the next town. But she wasn't microchipped, and then she just climbed on my shoulder and fell asleep and I thought, that's it, she was coming with me.'

He called his new stripy companion Nala and she

stayed with Dean for the rest of his cycling adventures throughout Europe and Asia. The pair are now social-media stars, and the video of how they met and the kindness of strangers along the way will melt your heart. 'She has taught me just to slow down and enjoy life a lot more. If there's woods we stop and play and she loves running on the beach.'

The real Puss in Boots

Puss in Boots was a character first concocted by Frenchman Charles Perrault, who included 'Le Chat Botté' in his 1697 collection of fairy stories. The Puss in Boots tale focuses on deception, lying and creating a better world for yourself – so far so good. A miller dies and leaves his three sons all his worldly possessions: his mill to his eldest son, an ass to the middle son, and his cat to the youngest son. Not being a huge cat fan, the youngest son thinks he's drawn the short straw – until the cat promises that if the son gets him a pair of boots, he will prove a worthy and helpful pet. And so he does, securing his master an arranged marriage to a princess and a kingdom to reign over. Phew!

Rescue wonders

Mike and Camilla O'Hara are cat people – 1,250-cat people in fact. Over the last ten years they have opened the doors of their Dubai mansion to all manner of abandoned, stray and injured cats. Even though their monthly shopping bill includes the cost of hundreds of kilos of food, they wouldn't have it any other way, both having grown up and looked after pets all their lives. 'Nineteen years ago, we rescued a cat, brought her home; then we got two more. In 2010 we moved into a villa and the rescue started to grow,' confessed Mike. 'At one point, we had over 100 cats living with us. That's just the scale of strays we find daily.' Lucky strays, we say!

Tom and Jerry

The most famous cat-and-mouse cartoon in the world features the domestic adventures of its titular characters, Tom (a cat) and Jerry (a mouse, who Tom constantly tries to catch). *Tom and Jerry* was created by William Hanna and Joseph Barbera and first shown in 1940; between then and 1958, the show's original run for MGM comprised 114 short films. Their plots generally focus on Tom's chaotic attempts to capture Jerry and the ensuing mayhem and destruction as Jerry outwits him through a combination of cunning, quick-wittedness and luck.

However, they sometimes show a fondness for each other – especially when they unite to assist supporting characters or to avoid mortal danger. Because of its limited dialogue, *Tom and Jerry* was translated and shown in lots of different countries worldwide. The cartoon proved particularly useful in the UK when the BBC had problems with broadcasts overrunning or shows being cancelled. For example, in 1993 *Tom and Jerry* was shown when a bomb scare at BBC Television Centre led to the cancellation of regular programming.

'My cat won't drink from a bowl, she will only drink tap water and will demand the tap is turned on for her every time I go into the bathroom. Her name, Seren, means Star in Welsh so obviously she likes to be a bit of a star-like diva.'

Cordelia Rhodes

Maru

Billed as the most famous cat on the internet, you might well be one of the many millions of people who have viewed some of his videos over 535 million times. We kid you not, the Scottish straight cat who lives in Japan with his owner holds the Guiness World Record for the most YouTube videos of any individual animal. His videos feature him up to various feline pursuits including playing with a box and he has also released a book, *I Am Maru*, a DVD and a second book, *More Maru*. Could there be a more famous kitty?

Trains for Tama

A young calico cat called Tama lived near Kishi Station, the final of fourteen stops on a busy railway line in Japan, and loved hanging out by the station to receive daily affection from the weary commuters. Over the years she was referred to as Kishi's stationmaster and was later given a customised stationmasters hat. She was officially named 'Stationmaster of Kishi Station' in 2007 and in promotional material and media coverage as the 'feline face' of the railway. She didn't get a salary but instead all the cat food she needed and Tama was so adored that even when she died, a painted portrait of her was soon commissioned. It currently hangs alongside other pawfectly posed photos of her in Kishi Station's souvenir shop where visitors can buy everything from Tama badges and keyrings to Tama-branded confectionary.

Grumpy Cat

Grumpy? Moi? Never has a cat's face summed up so many moods so brilliantly more than Grumpy Cat, whose real name was Tardar Sauce. She first found fame with her cantankerous face when a photo of her was posted on social news website Reddit in 2012. Then her crabby cat face soon hit the big time and she had her own internet meme – the accolade of few. Grumpy Cat had a record number of followers on social media too, over 1 million on X (formerly known as Twitter), over 8 million on Facebook and over 2 million on Instagram. All because (and thanks to her feline dwarfism and underbite) she looked like she was the original cranky cat.

Play it again, Keyboard Cat

Probably the best thing about the internet (and we know you'll agree) is the cat videos. And for the many millions we have now to enjoy there was perhaps, a piano playing cat that started the trend off, an overweight orange tabby called Fatso. In 1984 Fatso's owner recorded a video of the cat seemingly playing a jaunty tune on the keyboard while wearing a T-shirt. Fast-forward to 2007 (Fatso had died in 1987) and he uploads the video to YouTube and then, a couple of years later, gives permission for his cat video to be part of an entertainment channel that sees him 'playing off' footage of someone tripping and falling down an escalator. And that my friends, is how a viral sensation was born.

Long-haired Colonel

With a Guiness World Record for the longest hair on a cat, you might be forgiven for thinking Colonel Meow was a bit of a pampered, prima donna puss. But the Himalayan cross-breed, who lived in America with his owners, was more lovingly known by his followers (and he had a fair few on social media) as a bit of a scowler. And that's putting it mildly, as he was actually often referred to as an 'adorable fearsome dictator' or 'a prodigious Scotch drinker'. Oh, and 'the angriest cat in the world' was also a favourite label.

Super-cat Tara

Not many cats would be worthy of superhero status but Tara the tabby cat from California in the United States deserves just that. In 2008 video surveillance footage, she chased off a neighbour's dog who was attacking her human family's little boy Jeremy on the driveway. She managed to scare and chase off the dog who had the four-year old by his leg and then went back to sit with him until help arrived. When the video was uploaded to YouTube it received over 16 million views in the first forty-eight hours and no one was in any doubt as to who to call when there was trouble in their neighbourhood. Tara the hero cat.

Hey Bubba

Lil Bub – so called as when her owner first picked her up as the runt of the litter, he said, 'Hey bub' – was a famous America celebrity cat because of her unique look. When photos of her first appeared on the internet in 2011, people couldn't get enough of her face which was caused by several genetic mutations and meant she had to be bottle fed. It also meant, among other things, that she couldn't keep her tongue in her mouth. She went on to have over 3 million followers on Facebook and would tour the US with her owner by having meet and greets at animal shelters, to whom they would donate a portion of the money too. She also met Grumpy Cat. Oh, and she had a book written about her too.

White Socks

Socks Clinton was the first feline of the White House when Bill Clinton was President of the United States in 1993. The Clinton family adopted the stray black and white cat after he jumped into the arms of Chelsea Clinton when she attended a piano lesson and since then, stuck with the family as they moved into the most famous house in the world. Socks was often taken on presidential visits into schools and hospitals and any young visitors to the White House website would be guided around the site by a cartoon version of the puss.

Cat chauffeur

Ever see a cat drive a car? No, us neither, but Cat Toonces was the pet of Lyle and Brenda Clark, who would always allow their cat to drive the family car. They were thrilled that their cat had such a motoring ability, but they were always horrified to discover that Toonces was actually not a skilled driver at all. And he would regularly drive them off a cliff. Fear not, this tale isn't real; Cat Toonces was part of a sketch that would regularly appear as a Saturday Night Live character, with comedian Steve Martin playing the role of Lyle. Toonces was played by a live cat for the close-up scenes but a grey and white short-haired tabby puppet which had his paws on the wheel for the actual driving.

The cat with no tail

As it so often is with animals who look a little different, they take up the most space in our hearts and Stubbs the cat is no different. In 1997, a shop owner found Stubbs in a box full of kittens that had been abandoned and took a liking to him because he had no tail. He soon became a bit of a character in the small town of Talkeenta, Alaska, and was awarded the honorary title of mayor. Most afternoons, Stubbs would go to a restaurant and would drink water mixed with catnip out of a cocktail glass. He became a tourist attraction for people en route to other Alaskan destinations who wanted to meet him – or maybe have a drink with the meowing mayor.

Hamilton's mouse

The humble tache has seen a bit of a resurgence over the years but a moustache on a mouse-catching feline? Let us introduce you to Hamilton the Hipster Cat who was born with a fur pattern that resembles the most stylish curled moustaches. He quickly became an internet sensation for that very reason as the most dapper kitty in the world, generating nearly 1 million followers on Instagram and raising lots of money with his owner for a particular charity – the animal shelter that gave him his fancy feline.

Popular cat names from the world of film and TV

Need some inspiration for the naming of your mog? Why not opt for a theatrical name from the world of film and television:

Richard Parker: After the large Bengal tiger in Yann Martel's *Life of Pi*. This would be an ideal name for tabbies of a dominating manner. The unusual name will make sure your feline gets the red-carpet treatment.

Simpkin: For the star of Beatrix Potter's *The Tailor of Gloucester*. In this story, Simpkin is the cat that catches all the mice in the tailor's shop. A perfect name if you have a cheeky hunter in your home.

Tybalt: This character was actually killed in Shakespeare's *Romeo and Juliet* (and is, of course, a human), but setting those things aside . . . Mercutio repeatedly refers to Tybalt as the 'Prince of Cats' in reference to his speed and agility.

Thackery Binx: Fans of the film *Hocus Pocus* will know that Thackery Binx was a boy who was turned into a cat by three evil witches after trying to save his sister Emily.

Minnaloushe: This was the name that W. B. Yeats gave the black cat in his poem 'The Cat and the Moon' (see Chapter 3: Poems, Paws and Prose). Impress your friends with this highbrow name if you too have a raven-coloured puss.

Mrs Norris: Harry Potter fans will know (but probably not love) Mrs Norris as the nosy cat that likes to prowl the corridors of Hogwarts and let out a loud meow when she sees students misbehaving. An ideal name for a cat that likes to be involved in everything and anything and hates being left out.

Bagheera: As the sensible panther in Rudyard Kipling's *The Jungle Book*, Bagheera is a wise soul who helps to guide Mowgli out of the dangerous claws of Shere Khan. Perfect for an older, wiser cat who has a good instinct and a calm manner.

Tao: In the book *The Incredible Journey* by Shelia Burnford, Tao is a Siamese cat who, along with his two canine companions Bodger and Luath, travels for miles looking for their long-lost family. Tao is loyal, a fierce hunter and a devoted friend.

Garfield: Perfect if you have a ginger cat with a big attitude, the name Garfield could be used in tribute to the famous cartoon character. It's rumoured that Garfield's creator, Jim Davis, used the name Garfield in a nod to his grandfather, James A. Garfield Davis, who was a particularly large fellow with a cantankerous nature.

Bagpuss: The magical cat and star of the hugely popular English TV show of the same name, Bagpuss the old saggy cloth cat is owned by a young girl called Emily who shows him various items that need repairing each episode. If you have a cat with a big heart, is a little portly around the waist and perhaps not the prettiest of things, Bagpuss would be a perfect name.

Duchess: Before the hastag #catroyalty became a thing, Duchess and her trio of well-to-do kittens were the stars of Disney's *The Aristocats*. Duchess wore a diamond encrusted collar but was never showy-off about her status which is rather handy as she fell in love and got together with alley cat Thomas O'Malley. And they lived happily ever after, of course. Duchess is probably fit for any female feline.

There are lots of cat characters that have made their mark in the world of TV and film, animations and newspaper cartoon strips. Whether you want to name your feline after one of the fictional cats we have already listed above or just want to check out and appreciate more fabulous felines, we are feeling like the cat that got the cream with the following directory:

Felix the cat: One of the most recognised cartoon cats of all time, Felix, the young black cat with big white eyes and giant smile, was a character created in 1919 during the silent-film era. The name Felix was used after the Latin words *felis* for cat and *felix* which means happy. Sounds like the perfect name to us!

Hello Kitty: The cute white cat with the red bow was the creation of designer Yuko Shimizu, and when she first appeared on merchandise in 1975, immediately sold well. She was affordable and the Hello Kitty products, which saw a huge increase in popularity with the 'cuteness' trend in the early '90s, saw her popularity rise to great prominence. Having first been targeted at children and pre-teens, Hello Kitty was later marketed at an older audience as a retro brand. Mariah Carey was a fan so you know she was one popular Kitty.

Top Cat: Top Cat, or TC to his pals, is the leader of a gang of Manhattan alley cats in the cartoon series of the same name. Top Cat and his gang were inspired by the street-smart characters of the East Side and the plots each episode usually revolve around them trying to outwit police officer Dibble. He spends his time either trying to arrest them or evict them or get them to clean the alley – all of which regularly fail.

Heathcliff: Dubbed the original ginger cat, Heathcliff appeared in a newspaper comic strip from 1973. Which means he is the original orange tabby who likes to menace dogs a few good years before Garfield came along. And yes, he was named after the character in Emily Brontë's classic tale, *Wuthering Heights*.

ThunderCats: A popular cartoon in the 1980s, *ThunderCats* featured a group of humans who were also part cat. They had names such as Cheetara, Bengali and Lion-O and the action would revolve around them trying to defeat the evil sorcerer Mumm-Ra who wanted to take over the universe. Not on the ThunderCats' watch!

Simon's Cat: What's not to love about a fat white hungry cat who uses every tactic known to man and cat to get his owner to feed him? The success of *Simon's Cat* grew from a simple cartoon strip to a film to a book before he even had his own game released, *Simon's Cat Dash*. And yes, he did get fed too.

Catbert: The ruthless ginger cat who features in the comic strip *Dilbert*, Catbert is the company's HR manager and was only originally meant to feature in a few strips. But everyone loves an evil HR manager and Catbert is exactly that, creating ludicrous office policies while having his tummy rubbed.

Feline soldiers: cats in war

Here we introduce some of the most heroic felines you'll likely ever hear about. And you thought cats just napped all day – pah!

'One cat at the hole, and ten thousand mice dare not come out.'

Sun Tzu, *The Art of War*

The Crimean War

In 1854, British and French soldiers endured the hardships of Russian winter as they began a siege of the port of Sevastopol on the Crimean Peninsula. After a year, they were able to search the port properly and by that time were desperate for food. Captain William Gair came upon a very tame but abandoned tabby who seemed unaffected by all the chaos of the siege. The cat followed Gair back to the officers' shelter and became a favourite with the soldiers, who called him Crimean Tom.

One day, Tom left the shelter and led some of the soldiers to a pile of rubble, attracted by the rats that were living inside of it. Behind the rubble was a storeroom full of food that, until now, only this small feline had been able to access; but now that the starving soldiers were aware of its existence, they were able to make use of it. Tom continued to find hidden food storerooms by following the rats and became a celebrated hero among his regiment.

The First World War

During the First World War, some 500,000 cats were officially employed by British forces to serve as ratters and mousers in the trenches. They also alerted troops to the advance of poisonous gas clouds, saving thousands of lives.

A cat called Percy had a unique experience during WWI serving with his master Lt Harry Drader as a mascot in a tank. Percy accompanied Drader and the Royal Northumberland Fusiliers in their D20 tank ('Daphne'), which took part in the Battle of Ancre, which was the last of the big British attacks of the Battle of the Somme. Both Percy and his master survived the War.

Lt Philip Gosse with the Royal Army Medical Corps 10th Northumberland Fusiliers wrote movingly in his war diary about how all the cats he saw in Flanders were 'poor skulking specimens of a noble race'. But there was one exception, a cat called Félicité, who he described as a small white and tortoiseshell cat who was very affectionate and confident.

Gosse would describe how she would sit on his shoulder while he was writing, 'forever whispering' in his ear, reading what he had written and purring loudly. She would also sleep curled up beside him on his bed which was a particular comfort. Cats who had lost their civilian masters would often be transient visitors to the trenches, offering both service as rat catchers and a source of comfort to those who missed home. Often settling in to become part of the fixtures and fittings of trench life, cats would offer homesick soldiers a great focus for affection and attention.

Gosse knew, however, that Félicité was an intelligent cat and that her fondness for him was probably due to the offerings he would provide her in the shape of a small animal carcass. 'Each day after I had finished skinning a mouse or a vole, Félicité would oblige me by disposing of the carcass,' he wrote. Nobody was more concerned with the success of each night's trappings apparently!

Sapper Albert Martin, 122nd Signal Coy of the 41st Division revealed that there was a black-and-white kitten that lived in his dugout and would be of 'common interest' to all the soldiers. But the remarkable thing observed by all who saw this kitten was that it could differentiate between the sounds of friendly shell fire and those of the enemy.

'Puss takes no notice of our guns firing, nor the sing and whistle of our own shells coming towards us from the rear but when Fritz starts to send any over to us, she makes a beeline for the dugout,' revealed Martin. 'She doesn't wait for the shell to burst, as soon as she hears its whistle, she's off and she won't come out of the dugout until the shelling is finished. There is something more than instinct in that,' he quite rightly noted.

'It's not possible to remember where I found my kitten. I know we had been on the go in the final push that beat the Hun out of France in 1918, on the go for days and nights,' recalled Lt Reginald Dixon, 251st Seige Battalion. Dixon spoke of reaching a farmyard in the middle of the night and as the sun rose the following day, spotted a tiny movement under the gun carriage between the two wheels.

'"Blimey, it's a bloody kitten!" I exclaimed, everybody could see what I had in my hands and it somehow cheered everyone up,' he revealed. Dixon then put the kitten into his trench coat pocket and continued to set up his gun before heading to the farmhouse kitchen which was being treated as a temporary mess. It was only when he sat down and had a swig of tea that he remembered about the kitten!

'I pulled the little beggar out, unsquashed with all its nerves intact and my fellow officers stood around and admired the mite of tabby fur and whiskers and made a fuss of her,' he proclaimed. A saucer of milk was produced and apparently the young feline, surrounded by the 'rough kindliness of gunner officers in full war kit, mewed for more'.

The kitten, or Mr Dixon's kitten, became famous in 251 Battery and, being cared and fed by him, accompanied him until he went on leave.

The Second World War

Cats deployed to hunt vermin in food stores during the Second World War were considered so important that they were awarded a powdered-milk ration in honour of their service. The United States later launched a 'Cats for Europe' campaign and shipped thousands of American cats to France for similar purposes.

A female tabby named Faith and her kitten, Panda, made headlines in London newspapers during the Blitz when they were discovered under the debris of St Augustine's church after it suffered a direct hit from a bomb. The pair had been hiding in a storage cubbyhole in the rectory basement following heavy bombing in the preceding few days. Faith was awarded a silver medal and a certificate to celebrate her 'steadfast courage in the battle of London'.

A black-and-white cat called Simon travelled over 144,000 kilometres (90,000 miles) in total with the US Fifth Air Force that fought in the Pacific theatre in the Second World War. He first climbed aboard a cargo plane in Darwin, Australia, in 1945, and developed the habit of hiding among the radio apparatus and appearing just as the engines started. In 1993, Simon's Dickin Medal was sold at auction for more than £23,000 (US $42,000).

'Unsinkable Sam' was the name given to a cat who survived the sinking of three ships during the Second World War and became a legend among sailors. The first name given to him, however, was Oscar, after he was rescued by British destroyer HMS *Cossack* following the sinking of the German battleship *Bismarck*. It's thought that the black-and-white cat was owned by a German crewman aboard the *Bismarck*; and when he was found floating on a board in the water, the cat joined the British Navy as their mascot. It was then that he was given the name Oscar, derived from the letter O in the International Code of Signals, where it is code for 'Man Overboard'. Oscar stayed on the *Cossack* until it was hit by a German U-boat but he survived that too and joined the surviving crew, who were transferred to another destroyer, HMS *Legion*.

Now nicknamed Unsinkable Sam, the cat was then transferred to the aircraft carrier HMS *Ark Royal*, which was then also torpedoed by a German U-boat. It sank slowly, which allowed all but one of the crew to be saved – along with Sam, who had been found clinging to a floating plank. The loss of *Ark Royal* also marked the end of Sam's life at sea. He saw out the remainder of the war living in the Home for Sailors in Belfast. He died in 1955 but his portrait hands in the National Maritime Museum in Greenwich.

'The cat does more for the war effort than you do. He acts as a hot-water bottle and saves fuel and power.'

Winston Churchill

Able Seacat Simon is probably the most decorated moggie in naval history. He was found on a dock in Hong Kong by a British seaman who smuggled him aboard HMS *Amethyst,* where Simon got straight to work as a mouser, leaving 'presents' of dead rats in sailors' beds. The crew loved the cat for his cheeky antics, and he even made friends with Peggy, the ship's dog. After a year at sea, the ship came under fire and Simon was wounded by shrapnel.

He was missing for eight days and when he reappeared the crew took him straight to their medic because his whiskers and eyebrows had been burned off and he was severely dehydrated. In his absence, the rats had seized their chance and infested the food supply. However, despite being injured, Simon got right to work, killing two rats during his first night back and slowly but surely, over the next few days, clearing the deck of all the remaining rats – including one particularly large specimen. The crew named him 'Able Seacat Simon', which was the first military title given to a cat, and he continued to bring a shell-shocked crew comfort on their voyage. Simon died from complications from his injuries but was buried with full naval honours.

The master cat aboard HMS *Western Isles* during the Second World War was called Peebles. He served the important job of mouser, keeping the ship safe from rodents that might chew through wiring or eat food rations. But Peebles had another important job, as entertainer for the men on the ship. In this role, much to the delight of anyone who came aboard, he performed a variety of tricks. For example, he was known to 'shake hands' with strangers who entered the wardroom and was able to 'jump through the hoop' of his humans' arms. This intelligent feline survived the duration of the Second World War on board the ship.

Tiddles the cat grew up with (four) sea legs, having been born on board HMS *Argus* before serving on HMS *Victorious* in his official role as the captain's cat. He spent his entire life on board aircraft carriers of the Royal Navy in the 1940s and sailed over 30,000 miles. His favourite on-board toy was the bell-rope and his legacy is one of the reasons that black cats are now considered lucky in the United Kingdom.

In Stalingrad in the Second World War, a cat called Mourka proved himself invaluable. As well as keeping rats and mice away from food supplies, he saved thousands of lives in his role as a messenger cat. The deadly siege of Stalingrad made it too dangerous for Soviet scouts to deliver messages directly from the battlefront to headquarters, but the commander at the front knew that Mourka was one solider he could rely on. The cat would always scamper to the kitchen at headquarters, so the commander gave Mourka to a gun crew stationed at the front and told them to start putting messages in the cat's collar and then let him run. For several months, Mourka carried messages in this way back to headquarters, where he was given lots of treats. But he disappeared on one fateful trip and his fate is still unknown – although his status as a war hero has never been in doubt.

Princess Papule – or Pooli for short – was a cat who was born on 4 July 1944 in the naval yard at Pearl Harbour. She lived and survived on board USS *Fremont* during many battles, including in the Marianas, the Palau group, the Philippines and Iwo Jima; but during such battles she would spend her time asleep in the mailroom. The biggest threat to her safety came from her fellow soldiers when the war was over and the ship headed home. Fearing they would be quarantined in San Francisco because of her, some sailors wanted to throw her overboard. Others wouldn't have it and she was guarded round the clock for three days until the ship docked. Pooli earned three service ribbons and four Battle Stars and lived a happy life after the war ended.

Sniffer dogs are now used in the military to detect explosives, but cats have their own built-in bomb-detector sensors too. Whether they are simply attuned to changes in atmospheric pressure or have a sixth sense, some cats are particularly good at knowing when a bomb is about to hit. During the Blitz, families living in London soon learned to follow their cats into air-raid shelters, saving many lives. Among the most famous cats was one appropriately named Bomber. Apparently, Bomber could distinguish between the different noises made by RAF and German aircraft from a distance – so when Bomber headed for shelter, his family followed.

The Iraq War

In 2004, American soldiers stationed in Iraq were joined in their tent one night by a kitten born on their base. The others in the litter had scarpered but this little one stayed with the unit, chasing off mice who would have eaten or contaminated the soldiers' food. But even more important than his role as a mouser, the cat served his soldier buddies as a friend and source of comfort; and so the soldiers named him Private First Class Hammer after the unit. When it was time for the unit to go back to the United States, Staff Sergeant Rick Bousfield wasn't going to let one of his team get left behind. He told a rescue group about Private First Class Hammer and what he had done for the unit's morale, and the rescue agreed to raise money to transport the cat to America too. Hammer lived out the rest of his days with Bousfield and his family until he passed away in 2015.

The Ukraine War

Ukrainian soldiers have found solace in the companionship of stray cats. The cats – some of them strays; some of them house cats rescued from shelled villages – are helping to boost morale and protect the homesick soldiers who are living and fighting in the area. In turn, the cats are looked after by the soldiers, who share some of their food with the lost moggies. One military medical attendant has said the cats 'are like an anti-depressant – they lift your mood. You call them, and a whole swarm of them comes running your way. And you immediately feel better.'

Gorilla and Kitten BFFs

In 1983, Koko, the gorilla who had been taught sign language as part of a huge research project at The Gorilla Foundation, asked for a cat for Christmas. She kept signing the word 'sad' when she was given a stuffed toy instead and refused to play with the toy so the researchers gave in and let her choose a kitten from a litter for her birthday in July the following year. Koko selected a grey male Manx and called him All Ball.

Penny Patterson, who had custody of Koko and who ran The Gorilla Foundation, said that Koko cared for the kitten as if he were a baby gorilla but in December that same year, All Ball escaped from Koko's cage and was killed by a car. Patterson said that when she signed to Koko that All Ball had been killed, Koko signed 'bad, sad, bad' and 'frown, cry, frown, sad'.

Cats as Therapy

'Cats are my favourite animal because they love to cuddle with you and they are there when you feel sad or afraid.'

Chloe Harrison-Woodhouse

It should come as no surprise to us feline fans that cats are ideally suited to helping overcome emotional trauma, providing therapy and comfort to a range of people in a range of places. Specially trained therapy cats visit schools, hospitals and nursing homes in a bid to deliver comfort and companionship. Some of the benefits that people find with therapy cats include:

- Reduced stress

- Decreased symptoms of anxiety, depression and other mood and conditions

- Lessened feelings of loneliness

- Heightened abilities to form social connections

- A sense of calm

- An alternative focus to pain, anxiety and problems

- Feelings of surprise and importance

Cats can also provide that magic ingredient that can boost a low mood – the ability to make people laugh. The more people interact with cats, the more the feel-good brain chemicals such as dopamine, endorphins, oxytocin and serotonin kick into gear.

'A cat purring on your lap is more healing than any drug in the world, as the vibrations you are receiving are of pure love and contentment.'

St Francis of Assisi

Would Tigger make a good therapy puss?

Therapy cats are required to possess a number of qualities. Sure, we know that your cat likes to snuggle you, and not only when it wants something – but would it equally like to snuggle and be stroked by complete strangers, on demand?

Certain breeds are more adaptable to being trained as therapy cats, which means that they possess the following qualities: a calm temperament; being comfortable with new places; the ability to travel well; and a strong bond with their handler or owner. So, you know, it's quite selective!

The following breeds are best suited for therapy success – but if your tabby is reading this over your shoulder, they can be assured it doesn't mean other breeds don't offer love and affection and make suitable companions.

Maine Coon. Because these are naturally outgoing cats, they are friendly with strangers and have the ability to make us chuckle.

Persian. A favourite therapy-cat breed, Persians have the softest coats for stroking and burying your face in and bringing an overall sense of calm. Their chilled personality makes them perfect visitors and companions for both the elderly or younger children.

Ragdoll. Because ragdolls generally like to be around people, they will not think twice about sitting on the lap of a stranger ready for stroking. Gentle and kind, they are particularly good with older people.

Bengal. They aren't necessarily cuddly but Bengal cats are lots of fun as they have an air of silly mischief. They are perfect for entertaining children in tough situations with their ability to want to play over and over again.

Ragamuffin. Thriving on human contact, these cats are specifically suited to cosy snuggles, which means they are professional stress-busters. They should be renamed good-mood moggies.

'All cats are therapy cats; the majority are just freelancing.'

Lingvistov

Mental-health benefits of owning a cat

It's not rocket science. Catperts (experts in cats) can wax lyrical about why cat ownership is the cleverest thing a human can do to feel good. Preaching to the converted, here is our list of why having a purring companion really is the dog's whatsits:

You're no longer alone. A meow to greet you when you wake up, a cuddle at the end of a long day, a head nudging you around the legs as you wash up . . . The list goes on when it comes to the benefits a feline companion can offer. They are just *there*. They like hearing you talk to them. They like being around you. There is nothing like a feline friendship to give you a boost.

They are self-care reminders. You might want to stay in bed all day on occasion but when you must focus on the well-being of a creature that is solely reliant on you, you will eventually have to shrug off the duvet. A cat has a special way of keeping us on track, reminding us that they are number one in our lives ('Hello! Can you hear me meow? Shall I sit on your head again?') and that we are important in their worlds. And that makes us pretty important in the whole world.

They don't allow drama-llamas. You might be dealing with something that is hugely important at work; you might have had the mother of all rows with your bestie;

you might even have forgotten to pay the bills and find the walls of your house are crashing down around you . . . But there is nothing a nonplussed puss won't put into perspective. They couldn't care less about your drama; *they* are the only important thing in your life. Deal with it.

They turn us into relationship queens or kings. It's likely that, as a cat owner, you will have picked up on one or two traits from your feline friend. You are probably very sensitive to feelings, you are more open-minded, you are more trusting and, of course, you are highly intelligent. You are the boss of the dating world (partly/mainly) because of your moggy.

They boost our self-esteem. Having a cat that has chosen you as their master, has chosen your lap to be stroked upon, has chosen your head to sit on and has chosen your curtain to scratch makes you impressive. The cat has confidence in your abilities to look after it, so make sure you take some of that confidence to other areas of your life. Knowing that your cat is seeking out attention from you – yes, you! – is like winning life's lottery.

Cats who grieve

Grief isn't a concept that is exclusive to humans. Our cats are intuitive creatures and they too feel upset and can mourn the death of one of their feline companions or, of course, two-legged family members.

Cats' behaviour may change when there has been a recent loss in the family. Signs to look out for include:

- Loss of appetite

- Listlessness and no urge to play

- Sleeping more than usual

- Sulking or moving slowly around the house

- Hiding under the bed or choosing to be in an isolated spot more than usual

- Conversely, becoming clingier

- Changes in vocal patterns – for example, more meowing or howling or being quieter than usual

There are lots of ways you can help your cat overcome its grief. These include:

Spending more time with your cat. In theory this shouldn't be difficult but it is super important to help your cat feel comforted. Cuddle or play with them and if they usually like to socialize, invite your friends around. A little human variety can pique your feline's interest.

Being more affectionate. Again, this likely isn't going to be tricky but is super important. They will want extra love, extra strokes, extra eye contact and extra dialogue even when you are doing mundane chores.

Providing entertainment for them when you go out. This could include hiding treats in their favourite snooze spots around the house or buying some playthings such as foraging toys that require a bit of mental stimulation and keep them focused.

Keeping your behaviour boundaries clear. It might feel like the kindest thing to do, but reinforcing inappropriate 'mourning' behaviour isn't going to help you or kit-kat in the future. Tempting as it may be to reward an extra loud and soulful meow with a treat (for no apparent reason), your cat will quickly learn to repeat the noise if it leads to rewards. Instead, be firm in your 'Shhh' and praise them for being quiet – with either a treat or a cuddle. No one appreciates extra cattitude in their lives.

Speaking to a vet. If you find your moggy is mournful for a prolonged period of time, you might find it helpful to speak to a professional about options for medication and enhanced efforts to resolve issues associated with mourning.

Leaving enough time before replacing their lost companion. You might think that getting a replacement or new companion for your mourning cat is a good idea but this could potentially add more anxiety and upset to an already stressful situation. Give your moggy and yourself time. Cats have a much smaller social structure than we do, so losing someone or something from within it will leave a much bigger hole.

The sleeping cat

Cats are masterful sleepers, even from birth. Newborn kittens sleep almost 90 per cent of the time and even adult cats are asleep for approximately 60 per cent of their lives. Therefore, a fifteen-year-old cat has spent some nine years of its life sleeping!

'Cats are rather delicate creatures, and they are subject to a good many ailments. But I never heard of a cat suffering from insomnia.'

Joseph Wood Krutch

While cats are sleeping, they are still alert to external stimuli. If you disturb the tail of a sleeping cat it will respond accordingly. During a period of deep sleep, a cat may twitch its whiskers, flex its paws or move its tail. Scientists who have studied the amount of electrical activity in cats' brains during sleep agree that cats must dream.

Dreaming of cats

We know that cats dream as a way of processing all the information they have encountered – in a similar way that dreams are an important tool for humans. But what does it mean for you if your feline friends join you in the land of zzz?

The reasons you are dreaming of moggies can vary by the type of cat that features, so here's a quick run-down of what each one might mean:

Fluffy cats symbolize peace and relaxation. Be it a Maine Coon, a Persian, a Birman or a Ragdoll puss, if you dream of an unusually fluffy cat, you're looking for more peace in your own life. Particularly if you are always thinking of other people before yourself. Perhaps it's time to prioritize yourself for a bit. If the fluffball of your dreams is small and especially cute, it might symbolize a yearning for parenting or an emotional connection with someone.

Stray cats may signify loneliness. Are you feeling isolated in some way in your life? Do you yearn for companionship or company in a work or social setting? Seeing a stray in your dreams might indicate that you are feeling somewhat alone. Other interpretations signify that too often in life you let your head rule your heart – it takes a big heart to adopt a stray or rescue cat, so this dream is a reminder to you to allow your emotions to rule your brain.

'Never try to out-stubborn a cat.'

Robert A. Heinlein

Cats playing are a sign that you might need to rest. We know that cats are energetic and playful, so cats playing in your dream signify that you should try to imitate cats' other primary behaviour and relax. Take more naps! Alternative interpretations are that you are something of a naughty kitten yourself and may need to tone down your exuberant behaviour, or that you might be coming into money. So basically you should chill, be good or get ready for a windfall!

A cat talking to you means you should take heed. Talking cats (or other animals or inanimate objects) can signal communication from our unconscious that deserves our full attention. Much like when our cat companions demand we notice them, our subconscious should not be ignored. It may provide you with new perspectives when you wake.

Ferocious felines indicate a feminine connection. If you dream of angry cats you might be questioning friendship groups or your personal identity or have an unresolved issue with a strong female in your life.

Seeing cats everywhere suggests you have worries about the people around you. Perhaps you are wondering whether they are honest and trustworthy. It may be that people in your circle aren't looking out for you or supporting you enough, so prepare to confront such folk. Cats are quite often good judges of character!

Cat attacks relate to your inner thoughts and emotions. This is more likely to be a nightmare than a relaxing dream, and could be giving you the message that you should **pay attention to things** that only you know. Don't ignore the symbolism of the attack!

Purrls of Wisdom

'That awkward moment when
you're naked, trying to get dressed
and your cat is staring at you.'

Anonymous

The world according to cats

These are some principles that cats appear to live by,
wherever they are in the world:

There should be no closed doors in the house. To open closed doors, scratch and meow loudly. Once the door has been opened, walk away. A doorway at the front or back of a property is the ideal place to stop and collect one's thoughts. This is particularly important during very cold weather, rain or snow.

If you feel the need to vomit, make a dash for the nearest chair. If you cannot get to a chair, an oriental rug or shagpile carpet will suffice.

Computers provide many opportunities to be helpful. Jumping on keyboards, batting the cursor on the screen and lying in a human's lap to prevent them typing are all excellent ways of gaining your human's affection.

Repeatedly darting in front of cat owners improves their coordination skills. Particularly on the stairs, in the dark, or when they are carrying heavy objects or lots of shopping.

Given a choice of humans with whom to spend time, always choose the busiest among them and offer your assistance. If a human is reading, position yourself just between their eyes and the book. If they are reading a newspaper, jump on it. This will make a satisfying noise. Humans love to be startled.

Hiding from your human for prolonged periods leads to rewards. Occasionally, play a game of hide-and-seek by concealing yourself in a place where they will not find you. Stay there for three to four hours. Once your humans start to panic, come out and they will give you affection and possibly treats.

Advice for a kitten

Be prepared for a lot of attention. Like, non-stop attention, especially when you are first brought home.

There will be a lot of toys to play with. New toys each day, in fact, so explore them all. When no new toys are forthcoming there are some solid items around your new territory that can be easily played with; be sure to test them by clawing them first.

Humans like to show you off. You will be photographed constantly, even when sleeping. Be Insta-ready, always.

Humans will try to teach you things early on so go with it. But you can teach them about always being on their toes and getting your own way. For example, it doesn't matter if you go off certain food on different days; give them the eyes and they will bring you different food.

The middle of the night is the perfect time to find your human. They will love you to pounce on them and will scream with delight.

If you miss them when they leave the house, aim to sleep on them more. They will cancel plans/meetings/weddings with the proclamation: 'Sorry, I'm trapped under the kitten.'

'Kittens are born with their eyes shut. They open them in about six days, take a look around, then close them again for the better part of their lives.'

Stephen Baker

Advice for a cat

When you find sunshine, bask in it. You never know when it will be gone.

Ask for what you want every day. Loudly if necessary and at regular intervals. Your message will always be heard if you are persistent.

Take naps. And then take some more. And then when you wake, take another.

'A cat has nine lives. For three he plays, for three he strays, and for the last three he stays.'

American and English proverb

Move mindfully and gracefully. Sometimes the humans like to position obstacles in your path but you are soft and surefooted and nothing will get in your way.

Be focused and patient. You can watch a mouse for as long as it takes to pounce at the perfect moment. You are a master at this.

Stay alert and present in the moment while waiting for the above. The anticipation is part of the enjoyment.

Walk past mirrors with indifference. You know you look good.

Advice for granny cats

Sometimes it's just your turn to go to the vets. Put on your big-girl collar and go.

Never leave the house unbathed. You never know what Tomcat you're going to run in to, so it pays to keep yourself clean. We have standards!

Don't judge others. Your litterbox is just as dirty – you might think you are the cats whiskers but be respectful.

Be a connoisseur of comfort. You're an old and wise mog. You deserve only the best.

'The cat is, above all things, a dramatist.'

Margaret Benson

Share your wisdom. You've been around the block a few times and you know which neighbours will give you catnip, which ones have dogs and which ones like to feed the birds. Pass that knowledge on.

Play on your age. Food should be brought to you on a silver plate. Accept nothing less.

Timing is everything. You might want to run around and meow for no reason – but unless it's 2am, your efforts are wasted.

Advice for cat lovers

'A cat cuddle a day will keep
the therapist away.'

Henry J. Smith

'When a man loves cats, I am his friend and
comrade without further introduction.'

Mark Twain

'The cat has too much spirit to have no heart.'

Ernest Menaul

'No Heaven will not ever Heaven be unless
my cats are there to welcome me.'

Anonymous

'Never underestimate the power of a purr.'

Anonymous

'Time spent with cats is never wasted.'

Colette

The trouble with cats . . .

'Apparently, through scientific research,
it has been determined that a cat's
affection gland is stimulated by snoring,
thus explaining my cat's uncontrollable
urge to rub against my face at 2am.'

Terri L. Haney

'Cats can be very funny and have the oddest
ways of showing they're glad to see you.
Rudimace always peed in our shoes.'

W. H. Auden

'A cat will wait until you've read your
morning paper before tearing it to shreds.'

Anonymous

'You must set down all the rules to your cat at the beginning of your relationship. You cannot add rules as you go along. Once these rules are set, you must never, under any circumstances, break any of them. Dare to break a rule, and you will never live it down. Trust me.'

Kathy Young

'Cats have an infallible understanding of total concentration – and get between you and it.'

Arthur Bridges

'The trouble with cats is that they've got no tact.'

P. G. Wodehouse

'The trouble with sharing one's bed with cats is that they would rather sleep on you than beside you.'

Pam Brown

'How do cats decide when to jump suddenly
up from where they were sitting comfortably,
curled up, and dash madly around the room,
knocking over everything they encounter?'

Andrew Koenig

'There is no snooze button on a
cat who wants breakfast.'

Anonymous

'The problem with cats is that they get
the exact same look on their face whether
they see a moth or an axe murderer.'

Paula Poundstone

'Dogs eat. Cats dine.'

Ann Taylor

Why cats always come out on top

'If you are worthy of its affection, a cat will
be your friend, but never your slave.'

Théophile Gautier

'As every cat owner knows, nobody owns a cat.'

Ellen Perry Berkeley

'The cat stands alone, distinct –
out-individualizing every individual.'

Elinor Mordaunt

'It is perhaps easier for a cat to train a man
than for a man to train a cat. A cat who
desires to live with human beings makes it his
business to see that the so-called superior race
behaves in the proper manner toward him.'

Carl Van Vechten

'Cats seem to go on the principle that it never does any harm to ask for what you want.'

Joseph Wood Krutch

'Last year a team of scientists published the results of an extensive study of cat language. They determined that although cats may demonstrate a wide variety of vocalizations, they actually only have two phrases that are translatable into human terms: 1. Hurry up with that food. 2. Everything here is mine.'

Anonymous

'Cats never feel threatened. They are genetically incapable of accepting that anyone could possibly dislike anything as perfect as a cat.'

Kathy Young

'People who belong to Siamese cats must make up their minds to do a good deal of waiting upon them.'

Sir Compton Mackenzie

'It's really the cat's house. I
just pay the mortgage.'

Anonymous

'Cat: a pygmy lion who loves mice, hates
dogs and patronizes human beings.'

Oliver Herford

'There are many intelligent species in the
universe. They are all owned by cats.'

Anonymous

'Cats know how we feel; they
just don't give a damn.'

Anonymous

Cats versus dogs

Scientific tests in the UK have concluded that while a dog's memory lasts only five minutes, a cat's recall can be as long as sixteen hours.

'Dogs come when they're called; cats take a message and get back to you later.'

Mary Bly

'A cat's sense of taste is keener than a dog's. Cats are smarter than dogs. You can't get eight cats to pull a sled through snow.'

Jeff Valdez

'It's like I said all along: cats rule and dogs drool.'

Sassy, *Homeward Bound: The Incredible Journey*

'Cats are the ultimate narcissists. You can tell this because of all the time they spend on personal grooming. Dogs aren't like this. A dog's idea of personal grooming is to roll in a dead fish.'

James Gorman

'Even the stupidest cat seems to know more than any dog.'

Eleanor Clark

'When dogs leap on to your bed, it's because they adore being with you. When cats leap on to your bed, it's because they adore your bed.'

Alisha Everett

'While you might see a cat on a hot tin roof, a dog on a hot tin roof would be yowling its head off.'

Dr Bruce Fogle

'A cat I find [. . .] is an easier companion than a dog. A cat's sense of independence also enables oneself to be independent.'

Derek Tangye

'A cat will sit washing his face within two inches of a dog in the most frantic state of barking rage, if the dog be chained.'

Carl Van Vechten

'The dog for the man, the cat for the woman.'

English proverb

'By and large, people who enjoy teaching animals to roll over will find themselves happier with a dog.'

Barbara Holland

Cats versus humans

'I'm like cat here, a no-name slob. We belong to nobody and nobody belongs to us. We don't even belong to each other.'

Holly Golightly, *Breakfast at Tiffany's*

'Cats are much more at home in a warmer climate. They can tolerate a skin temperature of 126° Fahrenheit (52° Celsius) before they start to feel uncomfortable; anything over 113° Fahrenheit (45° Celsius) is too hot for most humans.'

Anonymous

'An ordinary kitten will ask more questions than any five-year-old boy.'

Carl Van Vechten

'A cat has absolute emotional honesty:
human beings, for one reason or another,
may hide their feelings, but a cat does not.'

Ernest Hemingway

'A cat's heart beats almost twice as fast as
a human heart – about 140 to 240 times
a minute in the average cat. If man could
be crossed with a cat it would improve
man, but it would deteriorate the cat.'

Mark Twain

'Cats are kindly masters, just so long
as you remember your place.'

Paul Gray

'A cat knows you are the key to his
happiness . . . a man thinks he is.'

Anonymous

'I've never understood why women love cats.
Cats are independent, they don't listen, they
don't come in when you call, they like to stay out
all night, and when they're home they like to be
left alone and sleep. In other words, every quality
that women hate in a man, they love in a cat.'

Jay Leno

'In a cat's eye, all things belong to cats.'

English proverb

'A cat has 250 bones in its body, compared to
206 in humans, which is why they can bend
and twist more than humans. If human,
cats might play solitaire, but they would
never sit around with the gang and a few six-
packs watching Monday Night Football.'

Time magazine

'I have studied many philosophers and many cats. The wisdom of cats is infinitely superior.'

Hippolyte Taine

'I love cats. I even think we have one at home.'

Edward L. Burlingame

'The playful kitten, with its pretty little tigerish gambols, is infinitely more amusing than half the people one is obliged to live with in the world.'

Lady Sydney Morgan

'Do I believe in love at first sight? Absolutely. I fall in love with every cat I see.'

Anonymous

Catvertising

Unsurprisingly, cats have often been used in advertising to promote products designed for their use. Famous examples of such 'celebrity cats' include Morris the Cat as the face of 9Lives cat food in the USA and, some years ago, Arthur, a white cat that ate with his paw in the promotion of Whiskas cat food in the UK.

However, since the early days of organized advertising cats have also been used to promote an enormous number of products aimed at the human market. Depictions of pet cats are often used to convey an idea of comfort and domesticity – take the fluffy, soft white kitten that featured on Dixcel's 'pillowsoft' toilet roll, for instance. Big cats like lions, meanwhile, suggest strength and power; and leopards and cheetahs represent speed, grace and beauty.

In Britain, the black cat is regarded as a good-luck symbol so, in 1904, Carreras introduced a brand of cigarettes called Black Cat, whose packaging and advertisements featured an image of a black cat in the hope that people would associate the brand with good luck. Carreras's cork-tipped, filterless Craven 'A' cigarettes also featured the head of a black cat on the packaging. The Black Cat brand was withdrawn long ago and the cat is absent from the Craven 'A' brand in its current form.

In the UK, advertisers eventually started to focus more on cat personalities instead of their cute looks. In 2002, a silver tabby was the star of the Barcardi Breezer adverts, which depicted the mog going clubbing and having a fun night out on the tiles before returning home in the early hours to sleep it all off. This daytime layabout with an active nightlife signifies the dual personality of the cat and young folk partying with a beverage or three. Cheers!

American superstar Taylor Swift is well known for her love of cats and her 2018 US commercial featured her two cats waiting for her in her backstage dressing room after a sell-out concert. The cats are mightily annoyed at Taylor for leaving them with just a few toys, a tableful of treats and the TV switched on to DirectTV Now for them to watch cartoons. Advertising genius. But that wasn't the first time she and her cat Olivia (just a kitten at the time) featured in an advert. In a 2014 Diet Coke ad with the slogan 'What if life tasted as good as Diet Coke?', Olivia appears to multiply every time Taylor takes a sip of the fizz. And then there was the famous 'cat-icorn' ad, again for DirectTV Now, which featured the singer sprinkling glitter as she rides on a giant Olivia – who has a rainbow-coloured horn – through a magical land. It ticks all the boxes.

A 2013 British ad for Cravendale milk with the slogan 'Jog on, kitties' features an unsuspecting cat owner pouring his cat's favourite brand of milk onto his morning cereal. Unfortunately, the cats in the street are all too aware of his crime and we then get to know what it's like when cats grow opposable thumbs. Watch out, folks.

One of our favourites has to be an American Electronic Data Software commercial that features a western-style scenario in which cowboys are herding cats. The sight of all those dirty and dusty cowboys embarking on 'one of the toughest jobs in the world' while sneezing, winding wool and rolling cat hair off their cowboy hats is just brilliant.

Believe it or not

Cat racing was once a spectator sport in England, though it wasn't particularly popular. The first official cat racetrack opened in Dorset in 1936 and took a very similar form to greyhound racing, with a number of cats chasing an electric mouse round a track. For one reason or another, however, it never captured the public imagination, and the last official cat track closed in 1949.

Cats are renowned for their ability to survive falls from great heights. However, studies have shown that cats falling from a height equivalent to eight storeys have a greater chance of sustaining fewer injuries, and of survival, than cats that fall from lesser heights. The theory states that once a cat has reached terminal velocity (after falling approximately the height of five storeys) it will spread its limbs and instinctively relax, and thus better absorb the impact of the fall when it hits the ground.

Dogs don't have a monopoly on loyalty to their owners and going above and beyond the call of duty. Stories abound of cats who have stayed by their injured owners, calling and screeching until help has arrived, or alerting family members during housefires.

Cats-concerto

It appears that musical taste is as varied in felines as it is in humans. Some cats show no interest in music, while others clearly adore it. A study conducted in the 1930s by Dr Morin and Dr Bachrach made the surprising discovery that the note E of the fourth octave made young cats defecate and adult cats become sexually excited.

'There are two means of refuge
from life – music and cats.'

Albert Schweitzer

Extremely high notes can cause agitation in many cats, and it would appear that confusion and distress occur because the sounds are similar to some of the 'words' in the feline vocabulary. Some of the high notes, for example, may approximate the pitch of the mews of a distressed kitten and therefore may disturb an adult cat, especially a female. An erotic response may be due to the similarity of the tones to the sounds made during the feline courtship ritual.

'I'm part human and part cat. Give me a radiator and preferably a human being to stroke my head and I'll be sleeping. If anyone wants to know where I am, I'm usually napping.'

Claudia Winkleman

What is the best type of music to play for your cat? Before you reach for the soundtrack from the Andrew Lloyd Webber musical (as if), you might investigate feline-friendly music. This is a genre created especially for cats and composed around their very specific hearing range. The hearing range for an average house cat is between 48 and 85,000Hz and is one of the broadest ranges among all mammals. Humans by comparison have an average hearing range of only 20 to 20,000Hz.

Cat shelters and rescues centres will sometimes play cat-based music composed specifically for cats to keep them calm and relaxed. If you don't have such a playlist to hand but want to find some therapeutic music, aim for classical, soft or gentle tunes and avoid heavy-metal songs with heavy vibrations of lots of bass that will play havoc with your cat's sensitive hearing. You'll probably notice their ears folding back before they scoot away.

A cat's tail

Tail facts

- A cat's tail is used primarily to maintain balance, and it contains almost 10 per cent of the total number of bones in its body.

- The domestic cat is the only species of cat able to hold its tail vertically while walking.

- It is a sign of affection when a cat winds its tail around something or someone.

- The tail plays a vital role in the 'righting reflex':

the instinctive ability that allows a cat to rotate while falling and to land on its feet.

Reading your cat's mood

A cat's mood can be read in its tail. You can familiarize yourself with this quick 'tail language' tutorial if you are unsure of what each position means:

- A tail held high and straight: 'I'm a friendly puss and very content.'

- A tail held straight up but puffed out: 'Back off, I'm scared.'

- A tail straight up with a curl at the end: 'You're my favourite person in the world.'

- A straight-up and quivering tail: 'I'm happy to see you' or 'I am about to spray on the furniture.'

- A tail pointed straight out behind when the cat is lying down: 'I'm relaxed.'

- A tailed tucked close into the body, between the legs: 'I'm feeling insecure or fearful; leave me alone.'

➤ A wagging tail: 'Now I'm angry. The more aggressive the swish, the angrier I am – watch it!'

➤ A slowly swishing tail: 'I'm loving this game with the sunbeam. I'm living my best life.'

Who doesn't love a cat idiom? Here are our top twenty favourites:

1. Fight like cats and dogs

A simile normally used for siblings who like to wind each other up continually. There is no winner, just constant, mindless bickering. It's not fun.

2. It's raining cats and dogs

Used daily by Brits who like to talk about the weather and who, of course, experience a high level of rainfall. Basically means stay indoors, you'll get drenched.

3. Herding cats

Normally an under-a-breath expletive ('This is like herding flipping cats!') and refers to a futile and exasperating exercise of getting people to move in a particular direction successfully.

4. A cat in gloves catches no mice

Be bold. Be brave. Take chances. If you don't, you're just like the cat who doesn't take opportunities and therefore doesn't get anywhere in life.

5. A cat nap

A short period of shut-eye that revitalises you into being the best person you can be afterwards. Try it. You are literally ready to rule the world after one (Napoleon swore by them).

'To assume a cat's asleep is a grave mistake. He can close his eyes and keep both his ears awake.'

Aileen Fisher

6. A scaredy cat

No one wants to be called a scaredy cat (see also no.4) but hey, when you're not feeling brave it's a fitting description. Besides, not doing a parachute jump doesn't make you a scaredy cat; it makes you pretty flipping sane.

7. Catfight

'Oooh, don't get your claws out,' or 'You're getting a bit catty,' are often used in reference to women having a barney – or catfight. It can be high-pitched and feral. But no one's perfect.

8. Cat got your tongue?

That moment when you can't get a peep out of someone who is usually very vocal/opinionated/chatty. Can be caused by a number of issues – feeling guilty, seeing someone attractive, holding back an angry retort (usually very handy that cat is holding said tongue).

9. Cat on a hot tin roof

Imagine you are very nervous. Anxious. Worried about something that's about to happen. Just like the cat, basically (not to be confused with the Tennessee Williams play).

10. Cat and mouse

Perhaps sounds more dangerous than it is, playing a game of cat and mouse means toying with someone, leading them on a bit and ultimately tricking them. Not to be played with a toddler.

11. Curiosity killed the cat

A good warning for anyone who thinks that confronting/ asking/enquiring/generally talking to a person with a resting bitch face is a good idea. It will never end well.

12. Don't let the cat out of the bag

Can you keep a secret? If the answer is no, you are like the unscrupulous farmer who would trick buyers into thinking they were buying a piglet in a bag only to find it was a feral cat. So basically you blab for England.

13. Like the cat that got the cream

Someone who looks like this is going to be smug/ pleased with themselves/a little bit superior. They have done something they are completely self-righteous about and want the world to know.

14. Look what the cat dragged in

Complete opposite to no.13, this describes someone who has been AWOL and looks rather sheepish or is, in fact, looking like they have had a rather fun evening and forgotten that they are responsible cat owners who shouldn't neglect their duties no matter how cheap the cocktails are.

15. No room to swing a cat

In terms of property in cities, the rule tends to be the more expensive or overpriced a dwelling is, the smaller it's likely to be. Literally, you have no room to swing a cat – something that we wouldn't ever condone even if you have the space.

16. Put the cat among the pigeons

It's not that we like a drama per se but if someone puts the cat among the pigeons – stirs up trouble – we will generally be found on the front row with popcorn.

17. The cat is out of the bag

Like no.12, this is the moment that someone with a big mouth spills the beans. Which is another ridiculous way of saying that the secret is no longer a secret. Everyone knows Majorie ate Karen from accounts' slice of carrot cake.

18. There's more than one way to skin a cat

Never to be mistaken for literal advice, this refers to the moment that a devious plan is foiled and you need to come up with an alternative arrangement. There is always another way to do something – or to skin the proverbial cat.

19. Not have a cat in hell's chance

Eat a whole packet of biscuits in under five minutes? No problem. Successfully binge-watch the whole four seasons of *Succession* in one sitting? Easy. Get a child to put on their school shoes? Not a cat in hell's chance.

20. Who's 'she', the cat's mother?!

A wonderful retort when someone refers to a woman as 'she' rather than their specific name; the woman in question can use the phrase (and it must be said slightly sarcastically), 'Who's "she"? The cat's mother?!'

Conclusion: You Had Me at Meow . . .

From highbrow poetic pleasures to the stars of mainstream commercial advertising; from symbols of wealth and good luck to heroic mousers during fierce conflicts; from ancient Egyptian goddesses to the cat mum in the flat around the corner . . . This anthology of cats has brought together a whirlwind paw-trodden journey of the history, the magic and the mystery of our feline friends. Because cats are our thing.

It has charted their history and unique relationships with humans over hundreds of years and given you some weird and wonderful facts about why these furballs are the cats' pyjamas, why the therapy they provide can't be measured or equalled, and why their mysterious, beguiling qualities continue to intrigue us.

We must earn our cats' affection (which can be both successful and stressful in varying degrees), but in turn they soothe us during our most cat-astrophic days. We appreciate their honesty in showing us their emotions because we know when they are mad, bored and in need of some TLC and they appreciate us (most of the time) worshipping them. They love to laze and sleep in the sun or cuddle up with us on laps/ shoulders/heads – but in the next moment will smack us in the face and then scat-cat around after a single spot of light.

They are fluffballs of contradiction who demand attention yet offer the comfort that can't be found in any other place than their scratchy sandpaper lick. They live by the principle that it never does any harm to ask for what they want – a strategy that has evolved over time and across the continents. Their natural instinct to hunt has made them an invaluable asset to our survival; and, as any cat owner will attest, their desire to bring gifts on a daily basis is evidence that that hunter trait is still strong.

There are no ordinary cats. Their natural charisma ensures that everyone notices them; and as we all know, you can't out-stubborn a cat. The passionate quotes from the most famous cat lovers in history put the spotlight on their magic and how days, weeks and months can be spent procrastinating while work is to be done. They become the fluffy visual soul of a home, their purr the soundtrack to contentment. They are adored by the rich and famous and the young and old because they offer something – a chutzpah – that can't be measured or even suitably described. 'If you have a thousand cats, you'll live forever,' suggested one prominent American poet – and there is a truth in that idea that many would agree with. It's all about the cats. Which is, of course, something they have known all along.

'What greater gift than the love of a cat.'

Charles Dickens